Falun Gong

Maria Hsia Chang

FALUN GONG

THE END OF DAYS

Yale University Press   New Haven and London

Designed by Sonia Shannon.
Set in Bulmer type by Keystone Typesetting, Inc.,
Orwigsburg, Pennsylvania.
Printed in the United States of America.

Library of Congress Cataloging-in-Publication Data
Chang, Maria Hsia.
Falun gong : the end of days / Maria Hsia Chang.
p. cm.
ISBN 0-300-10227-5 (alk. paper)
1. Falun Gong (Organization) I. Title.
BP605.F36C47 2004
322'.1'0951—dc22   2003065148

A catalogue record for this book is available from
the British Library.

The paper in this book meets the guidelines for
permanence and durability of the Committee on
Production Guidelines for Book Longevity of the
Council on Library Resources.

10 9 8 7 6 5 4 3 2 1

To beloved friends who so shaped my life:
Susanna Fung (in memoriam)
Stephanie Free
Patricia Gayle Stephens

CONTENTS

ACKNOWLEDGMENTS

I owe many individuals my gratitude for their contribution to this volume.

To begin with are those who played a direct role in making this undertaking possible: John Covell of Yale University Press, who first solicited a proposal on Falun Gong from me; Professors John Copper, Chalmers Johnson, and Jan Prybyla, who counseled the press on whether my proposal had merit; Otto Bohlmann for his perseverance in obtaining a contract from the press and for his unfailing graciousness; and John Kulka, Candice Nowlin, and Lauren Shapiro for their patience and assistance.

To the two anonymous readers of my manuscript, I send my heartfelt appreciation for their criticisms, recommendations, and emendations, which vastly improved the final outcome. I am also grateful to the following individuals for their interest and moral support: my sister in spirit, Judge Patricia Stephens, for her prayers, steadfastness, and joy; my former students, Dr. Kevin Peek, Elfi Thompson, Jack Lambert, Angie Wise, Janet Hanifan, and Molly Raftery; Professors David Arase and Leah Wilds; my sister-in-law

Shireen Chang; and my father and mother, Pao-en and Huang-lu Chang. I have also benefited from the questions and insight of the students in my China course, especially Mary Payton and Anne Chen.

Lastly, but first in my heart, are my family to whom I owe everything: my husband, Professor A. James Gregor, for his peerless wisdom and certain discernment, and my beloved brood—Gabriel, Buffy, Michael, Charles, Raphael, Ariel, and Erasmus—for filling my life with their wondrous individuality and bliss.

Chapter One
A Religious Sect Defies the State

On April 25, 1999, a political earthquake shattered the tight control imposed by the Chinese Communist Party (CCP) over the vast lands of China. On that spring day, 10,000 to 16,000 ordinary citizens peacefully assembled in the heart of Beijing outside the party's headquarters at Zhongnanhai, the high-walled compound next to the Forbidden City where China's top leaders live and work. The crowd was well behaved and respectable looking, composed of women and men, young and old, including retirees in their seventies and eighties. From dawn until late into the night, they sat in silent protest, eight deep on the sidewalk, each clutching a small blue book. In their quiet way, the protesters managed to mount the largest demonstration in the People's Republic of China (PRC) since the 1989 pro-democracy movement.

The demonstrators on April 25 were followers of a spiritual sect named Falun Gong (Law Wheel Cultivation), also known as Falun Dafa (Great Law of the Wheel). The book they held was one of two sect publications, either *Zhuan Falun* (*Rotating the Law Wheel*) or *Falun Dafa* (*Great Law of the Wheel*). The protesters had come from across China to ask that their government accord legal recognition to their sect, lift its ban on sect publications, and release their colleagues who had been arrested the previous day for demonstrating in Tianjin, a city about ninety miles southeast of Beijing.[1] Thus it was that the world was introduced to a new religious movement that claimed a worldwide membership numbering in the millions.

That thousands of its citizens managed to elude its supervision to coordinate and assemble en masse in as politically sensitive a locale as the leadership compound both surprised and unnerved the Chinese government. More than that, the demonstrators included intellectuals, government officials, and even members of the Communist Party.

When Chinese Premier Zhu Rongji met with protest leaders that day, he was reportedly stunned to find among them fellow party officials, including a retired Railways Ministry officer.[2] More troubling still for the authorities was the size of the sect, officially estimated at 30 million adherents. The sect, for its part, claimed twice that number, which, if true, would make Falun Gong the largest voluntary association in China, with a membership rivaling that of the Communist Party. More than that, including its adherents in China, the sect claimed a total worldwide following of 100 million in such countries as Taiwan, Singapore, the United States, Canada, Europe, and Australia.[3] As the sect's founder put it, "I think the government's biggest concern is that the number of Falun Gong practitioners outnumbers the membership of the Chinese Communist Party. Even worse, Chinese Communist Party members are open practitioners of Falun Gong." Indeed, until it was banned, it was reported that Falun Gong devotees "could be found in almost every park and on almost every street corner" in the People's Republic.[4]

Falun Gong's Beginnings

Falun Gong was founded in 1992 by Li Hongzhi, a former minor provincial government official described by Western journalists who have interviewed him as baby-faced and peaceable.[5] Born in northeastern China in 1952, Li began practicing *qigong* (literally, energy cultivation) when he served on the park police of Jilin province in the 1980s. That decade saw in China an explosion of popular interest in qigong, an ancient system of breathing exercises believed to channel the body's vital energy to enhance health, prolong life, and enrich spiritual awareness and insight.[6] When the CCP came to power in 1949, it suppressed all autonomous voluntary associations, including traditional groups such as qigong. In the late 1970s, however, the party relaxed its control over society and lifted the ban on voluntary organizations. Social groups, including those on qigong, began to sprout across the country. By 1998, qigong affiliations numbered more than 2,400.[7]

The renaissance of voluntary groups and associations, however, was conditional in that they require the permission of the state for their formation and operation. After the bloody suppression of the 1989 pro-democracy movement, the Communist Party tightened its grip on all social groups. Through the Department of Civil Affairs (DCA), a centralized system of compulsory registration and control of voluntary associations was instituted to thwart the creation of autonomous groups by excluding those the authorities deemed undesirable. Once approved, a group's registration must be reviewed every year. In October 1998, new regulations were introduced to further constrict the registration process.[8]

China's political leaders initially supported qigong because they saw in it a solution to the country's health-care provision problem. Citing an internal government memo, a DCA official described Premier Zhu as being very happy about the popularity of qigong because such groups "can save each person 1,000 yuan in annual medical fees." Furthermore, "If 100 million people are practicing it, that's 100 billion yuan saved per year in medical fees"—money that the country could use for other purposes.[9] Moreover, some leaders personally took up qigong practice. It was reported that in 1992, none other than President and CCP chief Jiang Zemin invited a member of Zhong Gong (China Cultivation)—a qigong group that claimed a membership of 38 million—to treat him for arthritis and neck pains. Given that, it is all the more ironic that on February 1, 2000, the Chinese government banned Zhong Gong as an "evil sect," driving its founder, Zhang Hongbao, to seek political refuge in Guam.[10]

By 1992, after he was transferred to work as a clerk in Jilin's grain bureau, Li Hongzhi had devised his own variant of qigong, which he combined with elements from China's traditional creeds of Buddhism and Daoism to create a new religious movement—the syncretic sect of Falun Gong. He succeeded in obtaining official permission and registered his creation with the Qigong Research Association of China (QRAC), a governmental body that supervises all such practices. Li quickly attracted followers who revered him as master and whom he called disciples. By the mid-1990s, the sect had acquired tens of millions of adherents, its rapid growth facilitated by its minimal admission criteria, eschewal of membership fees, simple method of practice, and its founder's promise of health and salvation. As Li explained: "There are people practicing Falun Gong in practically every department and every province, from the highest state government to an average citizen, because it's not that the practitioners are intentionally conducting propaganda to ask you to come to learn Falun Dafa. . . . It is simply that someone gets ill and wants to do physical exercise. He feels that it is good, then naturally he comes to learn it. It's just like that. There isn't any formality."[11]

Reportedly, the middle-aged and those from the middle class comprised the sect's main following, although its ranks also included students and the elderly, as well as peasants. They came from all walks of life: teachers, physicians, soldiers, CCP cadres, diplomats posted in foreign countries, and other government officials. More than that, it was reported that among the followers of Master Li were the spouses and family members of some of China's top officials, including President Jiang, Premier Zhu, and officials of the State Council, the executive branch of the government.[12]

Li's title as the master and founder of the sect may give a deceptive impression of the degree of formal control he has. Reportedly, Falun Gong eschews any kind of rigorous leadership structure and is, at best, very loosely organized. Whatever organization there is seems to be in cyberspace. The sect is adept at modern communications technology; it maintains dozens of Web sites that make available Li's writings and provide a mode of communication for practitioners. Members also maintain contact with each other by cell phone, electronic mail, and the Internet.[13]

Before the government banned the sect in July 1999, Falun Gong enthusiasts would spontaneously gather in groups to practice their exercises in China's cities. In Beijing, as an example, there were more than 2,000 practice stations, each composed of tens to several hundreds of practitioners. As described by *U.S. News and World Report*, in one station in western Beijing, thousands of practitioners would line up in neat rows at 7 A.M. every Sunday to practice their qigong exercises. Harkening to the tape-recorded voice of Master Li echoing through loudspeakers, the assembled raised their arms together in perfect unison and, with their eyes closed, their hands swept slowly in a circle and came to rest in a prayer position.[14]

Falun Gong adherents also met in exchange sessions that were reminiscent of Christian fundamentalist revival meetings in the

United States. In one such session in an auditorium in Beijing, for three and a half hours, one devotee after another climbed onto the stage to testify before the nearly 2,000 assembled believers on their miraculous recovery from ailments. Forty-year-old Li Jining, as an example, moved the audience to tears as he recounted how he had been a successful composer until he came down with a cancerlike illness that confined him to a body cast. Contemplating suicide, he picked up Li's book, *Rotating the Law Wheel,* and instantly felt "like someone had put a plastic shield around me." Within months, he was cured. Another believer, twenty-six-year-old Wang Weidong, had long been a drug addict until he happened to open *Rotating the Law Wheel.* When he opened the book to the first page, he saw Master Li's face staring severely at him and he broke into a cold sweat. After reading the book over and over for four days without sleep, Wang was purged of his addiction and began a new life.[15]

The Gathering Storm

In 1996, *Rotating the Law Wheel* reportedly sold nearly a million copies, which both alerted and alarmed the authorities to the immense popularity of qigong groups in general and of Falun Gong in particular. Fearing that such groups might morph into political organizations, the authorities saw in their popularity the potential for rebellion. On July 24 of that year, in the name of combating the spread of superstitious and unscientific ideas, the government's Press and Publications Administration banned the sale of *China Falun Gong* and four other sect publications. At the same time, several disgruntled Falun Gong followers were encouraged to accuse their master of bilking the public. In response, Li withdrew his group from the QRAC.[16]

That October, Beijing hardened its policy toward all qigong

groups: Those registered with the state would be more intensely monitored and supervised, whereas unsanctioned groups would be hunted down and suppressed. Any large-scale practicing of qigong in public places must have the authorities' prior permission; violators would be punished. Furthermore, all activities that "disrupt the economic order" and "destroy social stability" were prohibited. In November 1996, the official Qigong Science Institute removed Li from its membership. Sensing that he and his sect had fallen into disfavor—and reportedly at the urging of authorities—Li emigrated to the United States in early 1998, where he has since acquired permanent residence. Using Queens, New York, as a base, he travels around the world to teach his exercise techniques and impart his moral-religious beliefs. His itinerary is a tightly held secret. Even his closest disciples maintain that they seldom know where he is and usually get no more than two days' notice of an appearance.[17]

Meanwhile, in Beijing in May 1998, an interviewee on a television program referred to Falun Gong as a "cult" (*xiejiao*, literally, evil sect or religion). Alarmed by that designation, more than 1,000 Falun Gong devotees surrounded the television station in protest, eventually forcing the station to telecast a more favorable program. The next month, on June 5, the government banned the distribution of two other Falun Gong books.[18] Later that year, about a hundred party, government, and military retirees who were sect adherents petitioned Jiang Zemin to legalize the sect, but to no avail.

On April 11, 1999, the government ratcheted up its campaign against qigong groups when a Chinese Science Academy physicist named He Zuoxiu wrote an article for an obscure magazine (*Science and Technology for Youth*) cautioning young people against qigong. Singling out Falun Gong for special criticism, the physicist called it a superstitious cult and a health hazard because adherents might forgo conventional treatment for serious illnesses. Falun Gong followers wrote a letter of protest to the editor, demanding the author's written apology for distorting the truth and damaging the sect's reputation. When the magazine refused to accede to their demand, some ten sect devotees, on April 19, launched a protest before its editorial office at the Tianjin College of Education. In the course of the next three days, the number of protesters swelled to 6,000.[19] When the city's public security police forcibly removed one of them on April 23, the protesters took their grievances before the municipal government the next day but reportedly were beaten by the police. Ten of them were arrested. That became the catalyst for the massive demonstration on April 25 in Beijing.

Li Hongzhi had insisted that all he wanted was "to teach people to be good" and "not to be involved in politics."[20] Despite his sect's self-avowed apolitical nature, the simple fact of the matter is that by converging in thousands before the Communist Party compound on April 25, 1999, Falun Gong effectively became politicized because all demonstrations are forbidden in China unless they have state permits. That act of defiance precipitated the government's subsequent crackdown, the intensity and brutality of which have astounded and baffled the world.

The Crackdown

For three months after the April 25 demonstration, China's security services infiltrated the sect with government agents who clandestinely videotaped the exercise sessions. Jiang Zemin was reportedly obsessed with the sect and personally ordered the investigation. On the day of the demonstration, he asked to be driven around Zhongnanhai in his limousine and stared at the throng through the tinted windows. That night, clearly alarmed by the demonstration, he wrote the CCP Politburo to assure his colleagues that he believed "Marxism can triumph over Falun Gong."[21]

The crackdown began with a ban on and confiscation of Falun Gong's cassette tapes, videotapes, and publications. On June 10, 1999, a special task force was created to oversee the campaign. Named for the day of its creation, Office 6–10 issued detailed instructions to deal with the sect: active practitioners were to be sent to prison or labor camps; those who refused to renounce their beliefs were to be isolated and watched over by their families or employers. Local government officials were given carte blanche authority to implement the central government's directives. No questions would be asked about how this was achieved; success was all that mattered. If they failed to stem the flow of protesters to Beijing, however, local officials would be held personally responsible. In effect, they had every incentive to suppress Falun Gong in an unrestrained manner, a situation that could lead to great abuses of power.[22]

On July 19, 1999, the police seized literature and busts of Li Hongzhi and arrested 70 alleged sect leaders. Two days later, some 30,000 Falun Gong devotees staged nonviolent protests in thirty cities across China. According to eyewitnesses and human rights groups, more than a thousand of them were rounded up by the police. In Beijing, for example, demonstrators were forced onto buses and detained in stadiums. One eighty-year-old follower described an incident in Dalian city in which about a hundred practitioners were assaulted violently by the police. "This is the first time for me to see policemen beat people like this," he said. "All practitioners followed Master Li's teaching of endurance and suffered silently. We tried to be good people. You shouldn't beat us."[23]

The following day, July 22, the Chinese government identified the April 25 demonstration at Zhongnanhai as the most serious incident since the pro-democracy protests in Tiananmen Square a decade earlier. Despite the fact that the Falun Gong protesters neither carried posters nor chanted political slogans of revolution, they were declared an "evil sect" and banned as a threat to social stability and to "the vanguard role and purity" of the Communist Party. Even the private practice of Falun Gong was prohibited. The sect was accused of "conducting illegal activities, spreading superstitious, evil thinking," and stirring up trouble, its followers denounced on state television as fanatics driven to kill themselves and their family members. Communist Party members were ordered not to join the sect; those who did would be summarily expelled from the party.[24]

All over China, in scenes reminiscent of the feverish Great Proletarian Cultural Revolution (1966–69), police rounded up thousands of Falun Gong practitioners, some of them top party officials. They were brought to sports stadiums where they were interrogated, sometimes for hours, and forced to sign letters disavowing the sect. Local authorities from Beijing to Inner Mongolia ransacked the homes of suspected sect leaders, pulping or crushing with steam rollers more than 2 million books and instructional tapes. The homes of thousands of sect adherents who had been arrested and rearrested were put under police surveillance. As if that were not enough, economic sanctions were imposed on the family members of recalcitrant followers. They were threatened with dismissal from their jobs at state-run enterprises and government institutions, having their salaries and retirement pay withheld, and their promotions, health care, and education benefits denied. An arrest warrant was issued for Li Hongzhi, who was charged with enriching himself with heretical publications, disturbing public order by organizing mass demonstrations, and being an agent of the U.S. Central Intelligence Agency. A $6,000 reward (50,000 yuan)— a sum greater than six years' salary for the average Chinese urban worker—was offered for information leading to his arrest. Since the United States has no extradition treaty with China, Beijing requested assistance from Interpol, the international police agency based in Lyon, France. Interpol, however, turned down the request, saying that its constitution forbade it from undertaking "any intervention or activities of a political or religious nature."[25]

Government propaganda saturated the Chinese media with horror stories about Falun Gong practitioners, such as the teenager who allegedly killed his parents with a foot-long knife because he thought they were demons. Newspaper writers searched for new ways to vilify the group and its founder, calling Li's teachings "spiritual opium" and "an evil force" that must be "exorcized." It was claimed that Li had led more than 1,400 followers to madness. More than that, Beijing also accused the sect of purloining fifty-nine classified government documents and of being bent on destroying the social stability of China.[26]

An editorial in the official *People's Daily* called for "a serious ideological and political struggle" to combat this "evil cult." Falun Gong Web sites were blocked from Chinese Internet servers. Several sites reported being hacked into; one hacking attempt against a site in Maryland was traced to a police office in Beijing. Reportedly, 1,200 government officials who were followers were arrested; hundreds of soldiers and CCP members who were practitioners were dispatched to reeducation seminars to "study theories, refute fallacies, distinguish between right and wrong, and foster healthy trends."[27]

By August 1999, *Time* magazine reported that the Chinese government's crackdown had succeeded in intimidating Falun Gong adherents from exercising in public parks. Many followers temporarily left their homes; those who stayed waited for a knock on the door. Others were less fortunate. For example, the mother of Sophie Xiao, a Falun Gong spokeswoman and investment analyst living in Hong Kong, was repeatedly interrogated about the sect's organizational structure. After being detained and interrogated for forty-four hours, she finally recanted. Another follower, Huang Jinchun, a thirty-five-year-old judge for the Intermediate People's Court in Beihai, was detained for fifteen days for "damaging social order." A few weeks later, still refusing to renounce his beliefs, Huang was dismissed from his job and taken to a mental hospital where he was physically abused and forced to undergo psychiatric treatment.[28]

On October 30, 1999, more than four months after the crackdown began, Beijing sought legal legitimation for its campaign against the sect. The Standing Committee of China's parliament, the National People's Congress (NPC), met in a special session inside the Great Hall of the People to pass an anti-cult law restricting such religious cults as the already banned Falun Gong. The new law required that the courts, prosecutors, and police subdue any cult activity with severe penalties, including the death penalty, for cult leaders. The day after the anti-cult law was passed, the courts brought formal charges against four suspected leaders of the sect— one of them a former policeman—for organizing a cult and violating the national secrecy laws. On December 26, 1999, they were sentenced to eighteen years in prison after a one-day trial.[29]

The passage of the anti-cult law was supplemented by a revision of China's criminal code in November 1999, to formally designate Falun Gong a "devil cult" and, in so doing, render its adherents liable to prosecution for murder, fraud, endangering national security, and other crimes. The revision also enabled convicted Falun Gong followers to be sentenced to longer prison terms than those previously mandated by the criminal code for cultists. On November 5 and 6, 1999, China's official *Legal Daily* reported that Falun Gong adherents were being rounded up in Qingdao, Shandong, Xinjiang, Ningxia, and Liaoning provinces for "organizing illegal gatherings," "spreading antigovernment propaganda and illegal publications and books," and carrying out "illegal link-up activities."[30]

To prevent adherents from assembling in Beijing, the police made recourse to ordinances governing lodging in the capital. In one month alone, hundreds of adherents who had come to Beijing from the surrounding provinces were picked up in hotel sweeps and detained; landlords and hoteliers who illegally rented out rooms to adherents were punished with fines or forced out of business. The authorities also carefully distinguished between organizers and ordinary followers of the sect. In a November 5, 1999, circular, the People's Supreme Court admonished the courts to make a sharp distinction between criminal elements (sect leaders), who should be treated harshly, and common practitioners who should be extricated from the cult, educated, then reintegrated into society. On November 8, 1999, the State Council confirmed the arrest of at least 111 adherents for gathering illegally, "disturbing social order," "stealing state secrets," and other charges. Many others not formally arrested were administratively sentenced, without trial, by the police to reeducation through labor camps for up to three years.[31]

In effect, through such implementations as the anti-cult law, the Chinese government could now claim that its crackdown on Falun Gong was in conformance with the rule of law. Despite Beijing's claim, the activities for which sect members were accused—those of religious belief and practice; nonviolent assembly and protest; owning and disseminating books, tapes, and pamphlets; and using the Internet—are all clearly protected under international human rights law. More than that, in some cases, believers were punished for acts committed *before* the sect was banned. An example was Hu Qingyun, a high court judge who was sentenced to seven years in prison for helping a bookstore purchase Falun Gong books. But at the time when he allegedly committed the crime, Falun Gong and its publications had not been prohibited![32]

The Sect's Defiance

By April 2000, one year after the massive demonstration at Zhong-nanhai, Beijing claimed it had succeeded in persuading some 98 percent of Falun Gong's following in China to abandon their allegiance. At the same time, the government acknowledged that some diehards remained and that the struggle to destroy the sect would be "long-term, complex and serious."[33]

Those diehards persisted in defying the government's ban by undertaking bold acts of civil disobedience across China, especially in Tiananmen Square. Almost daily, some of them would penetrate the tight security around the square until the police arrived to carry them away. On April 25, 2000, the first anniversary of the Zhong-nanhai demonstration, about one hundred adherents made their way to Tiananmen Square in small groups. All were seized, most of them roughly, by swarms of plainclothes policemen and were subjected to reeducation. Those who responded well were treated leniently; those who resisted or were found to be ringleaders were put on trial, and eighty-four of them were sentenced to jail. On October 1, 2000, China's National Day, hundreds of devotees protested in Tiananmen Square and unfurled a banner that read "Falun Gong is not an evil cult." They were pummeled by police, arrested, and hustled into waiting vans. On December 10, 2000, about two dozen devotees appeared in the square chanting "Falun Gong is not a crime" and unfurled banners displaying the sect's moral tenets, "Truth, Compassion, Tolerance." Police ripped down the banners and herded the protesters into vans. On January 1, 2001, dozens of mostly female and middle-aged devotees gathered in the square to meditate and flash yellow cloth banners, but they were dragged way by hundreds of uniformed and plain-clothed police officers.[34]

At the same time as his disciples continued to defy the ban, Li

Hongzhi made increasingly urgent appeals on the sect's official Web site (www.clearwisdom.net), which took on political and apocalyptic overtones. In August 2000 he wrote that his disciples should "let go of all worldly attachments (including the attachment to the human body)," and that they must "step forward" and "achieve consummation" by facing imprisonment or death. When hundreds of them heeded his message and protested in Tiananmen Square on October 1, 2000, he responded, "I'm happy for those disciples who have stepped forward. . . . Whether they are imprisoned or lose their human lives for persevering in *dafa* (great law of the wheel) cultivation, they achieve consummation."[35] More ominous still, in a 2001 New Year's Day message, he seemed to urge his followers to escalate their struggle against the government. "The present performance of the evil," Li wrote, "shows that [the government is] . . . utterly inhuman and completely without righteous thoughts. So such evil's persecution of the *Fa* [law] can no longer be tolerated." Given that, the faithful could rightfully "go beyond the limits of forbearance" because tolerance "is not equivalent to doing nothing. . . . If the evil has already reached the point where it is unsavable and unkeepable, various measures at different levels can be used to stop it and eradicate it." He also anticipated that his disciples' struggles were leading to a transcendent event he called "the Consummation," in which only the believers would "leave" and those who remained ("all bad people") would pay for their sins with "horrible suffering" and "will be destroyed by gods."[36]

Frustrated by the sect's continued defiance, the Chinese government intensified its war by adding the crime of treason to the list of Falun Gong's offenses. On January 9, 2001, *People's Daily* called the sect a "cheap tool . . . of anti-China forces in the West" who were using the group to change China's political system. Politburo member Luo Gao asserted at a security conference in Beijing on

January 20 that Falun Gong had "degenerated into a tool used by hostile foreign forces" aimed at ruining China's reforms. Nothing less than the survival of the Communist Party was at stake.[37]

The government also fortified its legal arsenal. The Standing Committee of the NPC approved new rules defining illegal uses of the Internet and singled out, as one of the most egregious offenses, employing the Internet "to organize evil religious cults" or "for communications between cult members." On March 2, 2001, on the basis of those new laws, thirty-seven Falun Gong followers were sentenced to three to ten years' imprisonment for "using a cult to obstruct the law" by disseminating statements downloaded from sect Web sites.[38]

At the same time, the Communist Party government widened its campaign against the sect into a nationwide movement. The China Anti-Cult Association was formed to collect a million signatures in support of the ban. National television for the first time broadcast a videotape of Falun Gong followers protesting in Tiananmen Square and with bystanders deploring the demonstrations (the police's violent handling of the protesters, however, was carefully edited out). For its part, Falun Gong defended the continued protests. A sect representative in Hong Kong, Kan Hung-cheung, explained that "If they didn't repress us, there would be no need for us to stand up and tell the truth. . . . As the suppressions were so brutal and inhumane, we have to tell the world."[39]

On January 23, 2001, in Tiananmen Square, on the eve of the Lunar New Year—China's most important holiday—alleged followers of the sect undertook the most radical act of defiance yet. As described by a CNN television crew who witnessed the horrifying event (and whose videotape was immediately confiscated by the police), at about 2:30 P.M., five people doused themselves with gasoline and set themselves ablaze. One of them, a man who had been sitting on the ground, erupted into a ball of fire; the other four, two mother-daughter pairs, staggered about with their arms raised in meditative pose as orange flames leapt from their bodies. Police rushed to douse the flames and erected a shield to block the view of onlookers. One of the mother-daughter pairs, a thirty-six-year-old woman died from the burns.

The authorities immediately imposed the heaviest security clampdown on central Beijing in years. Checkpoints ringed Tiananmen Square, where police inspected pedestrians' identification papers, bags, pockets, and coat sleeves. In an effort to ferret out suspected sect adherents, the police harangued passersby to denounce the sect as "an evil cult" and its founder as "a bad egg."

Despite the heavy security, some of the faithful still managed to slip into the square. One man holding a banner climbed atop a mound of shoveled snow before police rushed at him from three sides, knocking him over. An officer pressed a knee into the protester's body, pinning him to the ground until he was shoved into a police van. Four other protesters were also taken away, including a man holding a red banner and another who yelled Falun Gong slogans as he was grabbed by three plainclothes officers. On February 16, 2001, another follower immolated himself on a residential street in Beijing. Sadly, by the time the police arrived minutes later, twenty-five-year-old Tan Yihui, a shoe shiner from Hunan province, had perished in the flames.[40]

China's state media at first made no mention of the fiery suicides. It was not until a week later that the government made the details public, with Central Television showing graphic footage of the self-immolations, followed by an interview with the heavily bandaged daughter of the woman who had died on January 23. Twelve-year-old Liu Siying said her mother fooled her into setting herself on fire, believing that, in so doing, they would go to the "heavenly golden" paradise that Li Hongzhi had described in *Rotating the Law Wheel*.[41] Xinhua, China's official news agency, said those who immolated themselves had been "hoodwinked by the evil fallacies of Li Hongzhi." It also claimed that another dozen sect adherents had committed mass suicide to attain "consummation" and that dozens more had been prevented from doing so by the police. For their part, Falun Gong spokespeople in New York and Hong Kong were incredulous, insisting that the immolators could not be followers because both Li and the sect had consistently opposed any form of killing, including suicide, as a means of reaching salvation.[42]

After the self-immolations, Beijing intensified its crackdown with a nationwide mobilization drive similar to those during the Maoist years. The campaign began with the arrest of five individuals for planning the self-immolations. All were found guilty by a Beijing court on August 17, 2001, for "organizing, masterminding, instigating and assisting" the suicides and were sentenced to seven years to life in jail.[43] Office 6–10, charged with suppressing the sect, issued orders to local governments and police to take all necessary measures against cult followers. The burnt girl, with her face charred and bandaged, was shown repeatedly on television crying for her mother.[44] The media was filled with invectives against the sect; an article by Xinhua carried by several newspapers had the headline "Li Hongzhi, why don't you burn yourself?" Schoolchildren were required to attend anti–Falun Gong classes; 12 million of them in a hundred large cities participated in a signature campaign and signed a "civil convention" declaring that they "don't believe in cults, don't spread their beliefs and spontaneously fight against them." Thousands of adults, from school teachers to steel workers, also attended mass meetings and signed petitions denouncing the sect. In recognition of their anti-cult work, citations were given to 110 organizations and 271 individuals; another 1,600, mainly members of the police and military, were awarded with large paper roses pinned to their chests. A Western diplomat compared the unabated and methodical campaign of suppression to a Russian pogrom.[45]

In the face of international criticisms and expressions of concern over violations of religious freedom and civil liberties, Beijing redoubled its accusation of the sect's foreign collusion. Two official newspapers accused Western news agencies and reporters not only of knowing in advance about the self-immolation, but of actively assisting in the suicides. On February 5, 2001, Beijing warned foreign governments against interfering in China's internal affairs "by making use of the Falun Gong issue." An article in the February 6 issue of *Legal Daily* called sect members "running dogs of foreign anti-Chinese forces," while the *Liberation Army Daily*, the mouthpiece of the Chinese military, in a front-page essay accused "Western anti-Chinese forces" of sparing no effort "to engage in ideological infiltration to achieve their goal of overturning our socialist system and subverting our state." The essay insisted that "what Li Hongzhi and his Falun Gong are attempting is precisely what the Western anti-Chinese forces scheme at." Members of the foreign press corps in Beijing came under increasing surveillance. Plainclothes security officers followed selected reporters on foot, by car, and by motorcycle; guards at commercial and residential complexes harangued reporters about their comings and goings and conducted repeated "smoke alarm checks" on their offices.[46]

Among the foreign anti-Chinese forces, the United States was singled out for special condemnation. Shanghai's *Liberation Daily* accused Washington of supporting the sect "to distract China's attention from economic construction and destablize the country." On March 7, He Zuoxiu, the physicist whose magazine article provoked Falun Gong's massive demonstration at Zhongnanhai, accused hard-core sect members of being paid professionals in the service of the American government. Speaking before the science panel of the Chinese People's Political Consultative Conference (CPPCC), an advisory body to the parliament, the physicist claimed that the U.S. Congress had given "several tens of millions of dollars to Falun Gong for activity funds out of ulterior motives."[47]

Taiwan was also a target of Beijing's invectives. On March 25, Beijing accused the authorities on Taiwan, specifically Vice President Annette Lu, of using the sect "for their own separatist purposes" to promote Taiwanese independence. (Falun Gong claimed to have about 100,000 followers in Taiwan, where it enjoyed a sharp rise in membership after the group was banned on the mainland.)[48]

On June 11, 2001, Beijing implemented yet more new guidelines aimed at the sect. China's top court issued a directive citing specific laws that could be used by police, prosecutors, and judges to punish Falun Gong followers. For example, defamation or libel laws could be deployed against those who "attack President Jiang Zemin in their propaganda material or spray-paint names of police officers" who allegedly tortured sect adherents. The directive also stated that adherents who gather or provide information on Beijing's crackdown to overseas groups could be prosecuted under Criminal Law 111 for spying or stealing state secrets—egregious offenses that are punishable by long prison terms and for which the accused would not have the right of defense.[49]

On June 10, 2001, a new legal directive "on the punishment of diehard Falun Gong cult members" was jointly issued by the Supreme People's Court and Supreme People's Procuratorate. The directive went into effect the next day, targeting those who continued to distribute pamphlets and information about the cult. Under the revisions, cult members could be punished under subversion laws if they produced or distributed materials about the banned sect. Falun Gong adherents who organized, encouraged, or helped other followers to commit suicide or injure themselves could also be prosecuted for murder or "intentional wounding." On August 22, 2001, a court in southern China exploited the new directive to sentence Lan Yunchang to death for allegedly murdering a fellow villager with an ax as a way to attain salvation. The sentence was the most severe given to a Falun Gong adherent since the sect was outlawed two years earlier.[50]

Against the onslaught of Beijing's campaign, Falun Gong devotees did not relent. In August 2001, for more than ten days, some 130 adherents incarcerated in the Masanjia labor reform camp in Liaoning province went on a hunger strike to protest being held beyond their original terms. And although public protests had dropped off since the self-immolations, on the second anniversary of the April 25 demonstration, 32 of the faithful managed to stage brief and scattered demonstrations in Tiananmen Square. They were beaten and shoved into wagons by uniformed and plainclothes police; Western tourists who had taken pictures of the demonstrators were forced by the police to expose their film and record over their video tapes.[51]

Nor did the self-immolations cease. On July 1, 2001, nineteen-year-old Luo Guili set himself on fire on a city square in Nanning in southern China; he died the following day of severe burns and heart and lung failure. Xinhua did not announce his death until three weeks later, at which time Beijing claimed that Luo "was trying to burn off the evil hidden in his body so as to reach a higher level in Falun Gong practice."[52]

If Falun Gong had been apolitical in the beginning, it was so no longer. Its adherents posted handbills on power poles in Shenyang city and blanketed mailboxes in Beijing back streets with fliers disputing the government's account of the self-immolations and criticizing the government for neglecting poverty and unemployment.[53] City residents were bombarded with videodiscs and automated phone calls that played recordings attacking the government. Sect activists also took to hacking into television broadcasts. For example, in March 2002, seven followers were arrested for hacking into the prime time cable television programming of two cities in Jilin, replacing it with a pirate broadcast of Li Hongzhi that lasted for about ten minutes. The next month, on the evening of April 21, activists broke into the cable television system of Harbin and succeeded in disrupting its normal programming for several minutes. In June, activists managed to hack into a state satellite system to briefly beam their message to millions. On September 20, 2002, for their hacking, fifteen activists received sentences of up to twenty years in prison, comparable to the longest sentences meted out to political dissidents in China.[54]

The activists were encouraged by their master. On March 4, 2001, in a defiant message on the sect's Web site, entitled "Coercion Cannot Change People's Heart," Li Hongzhi seemed to urge his disciples not to bow to the authorities, warning that Beijing's sustained crackdown would fail to break the faith of "true cultivators" even if "many people have been beaten to death, beaten to disability, or sent to mental hospitals." Ten days later, in a statement read by one of his disciples at a ceremony in the U.S. Congress to honor religious organizations in China, which was organized by the human rights group Freedom House, Li invoked the image of a Manichaean battle being waged in China. According to him, the government of the People's Republic was a "wicked dictatorship" whose "evil nature" was being challenged by the "goodness" of Falun Gong.[55]

Falun Gong also became a test of Hong Kong's promised autonomy from mainland China. In contrast to its fate on the mainland, the sect had remained legal in the former British colony because the latter retained a high degree of autonomy as a Special Administrative Region after it was returned to China in 1997. As a consequence, the sect's followers in Hong Kong had enjoyed freedoms denied to their counterparts on the mainland. For example, on January 13, 2001, some 800 Falun Gong followers from around the world marched on a Hong Kong government building behind 120 women dressed in white—the traditional funeral color—to protest the alleged torture-killings by the mainland police of 120 of their confreres. The next day, about 1,200 of them attended an all-day conference at city hall to denounce Beijing's "evil" and "brutal" persecution. They also claimed that 12 sect members were denied entry by Hong Kong immigration officials, and that the authorities granted them a permit for the conference only after they had agreed not to show photographs of followers being tortured on the mainland.[56] The following month, sect adherents in Hong Kong published a booklet condemning Jiang Zemin as "the culprit responsible for oppressing Falun Gong" and an "autocrat" who was "harming" China and its people.

In response, Beijing began to exert political pressure on the Hong Kong government. On January 31, 2001, Xu Simin, a member of the Standing Committee of the CPPCC said that Falun Gong was neither a qigong nor a religious entity, but was instead a political organization. He criticized the Hong Kong government for being too lenient with the sect and urged that its activities be outlawed, as they were in Macao. On February 6, PRC foreign ministry spokesman Sun Yuxi urged the Hong Kong government to curb the activities of the sect to prevent Hong Kong from becoming "a base for subverting the central government." At the same time, pro-Beijing politicians in Hong Kong began calling for the passage of antisubversion laws that could be used against the sect.[57]

On February 8, 2001, Hong Kong's Chief Executive Tung Chee-hwa seemed to bend under Beijing's pressure. Recalling the self-immolation in Tiananmen Square, he referred to Falun Gong as a cult that had shown evil characteristics and must be closely monitored. In response, Falun Gong spokeswoman Hui Yee-han observed that Tung's comments could only incite hatred against the sect. Tung was also criticized by opposition leader Martin Lee of Hong Kong's Democratic Party for "exactly toeing the Beijing line." "We are worried," Lee said. "If we carry on like this, and the central government isn't nice to the Catholics, or Protestants, or the Buddhists, either, will Hong Kong call them cults, too?"[58]

On April 27, 2001, Agence France Presse reported that the Hong Kong government was preparing legislation to outlaw Falun Gong. Allegedly, Tung might use an anti-cult law that the French government was expected to enact in June. Two months later, on June 14, Tung seemed to reverse himself when he announced, in a question-and-answer session with legislators, that he had no immediate plans to propose such legislation: "I don't think that it is now the time to enact legislation. We are not at that stage yet but we will keep a close eye on their every move." He did reiterate, however, his prior characterization of Falun Gong as a cult, claiming that "it is well organized, it has lots of resources and it is an organization that has politics on its mind."[59]

The Killings

In the two years since the sect's sudden assemblage before the Communist Party's headquarters, international human rights groups estimated that some 10,000 Falun Gong followers had been sent to prison, labor camps, or mental hospitals. Another 5,000 refused to recant and were kept under surveillance; tens of thousands more were briefly detained in makeshift holding centers where they were harangued and sometimes beaten until they renounced their beliefs.[60] In an interview with *Newsweek* magazine, Li Hongzhi claimed that "some people have had their bones broken, and some have had their hair pulled out." The holding centers are "transformation centers" where local officials enjoy a free hand in implementing the central government's directives. Pulitzer Prize-winner Ian Johnson of the *Wall Street Journal* maintained that "it was at these unofficial prisons that the killings occurred."[61]

By April 2002, nearly three years since the banning of the sect, Falun Gong's headquarters in New York claimed that more than 350 of its faithful had died in custody or from official persecution. Independent human rights groups, including the Hong Kong-based Information Center for Human Rights and Democracy (ICHRD), put the toll at over 156. The sect also claimed that about 100,000 people had been arrested or jailed: Among them were at least 500 practitioners who were jailed, some 1,000 confined to mental hospitals, and 20,000 sent to labor camps without trial. The Chinese government, in contrast, repeatedly denied that any Falun Gong members died in police custody, explaining the deaths as suicides or natural deaths.[62]

One of those who died was Zhao Xin, a thirty-two-year-old assistant professor at the business college of Beijing's Industry and Commerce University who had practiced Falun Gong for two years. For that, she was repeatedly arrested, the last time on June 19, 2000, when she and twenty other followers were practicing their slow-motion exercises in a park. Zhao refused to tell police her name or where she worked and began a hunger strike. On June 22, detention center guards sent her to a hospital with three fractured neck vertebrae, minor head injuries, and breathing problems. After surgery and three months of hospital treatment, she returned home because her family could no longer afford the medical fees. She died on December 14.[63]

Another victim was Chi Yulian, the mother of a ten-year-old boy. On May 29, 2001, she was cooking in her kitchen when police officers stormed her home, handcuffed her, and threw her onto her bed. The officers searched the house, and after they found sect-related material, they dragged her barefoot to a waiting police car and, from there, to a detention center. One week later, an official at the center informed her husband that she had had a heart attack and died on the way to the hospital.[64]

Other victims include the following:

- Fifty-year-old school teacher An Xiukun, who was detained by police and choked to death in June 2000 when police forcibly fed her.

- Thirty-five-year-old Gong Baohua, arrested at a demonstration in June 2000 in Beijing, had her nose broken by the police, and later choked to death at a detention center from being force-fed with a nasal feeding tube.

- Twenty-eight-year-old Li Mei, sentenced in June 2000 for two years to a labor camp in central Anhui province for protesting against the government's ban, was found dead with gauze bandages wrapped around her neck, her face covered with bruises and traces of blood from her nose.

- Xuan Chengxi was killed in October 2000 by the police of Weifan, a city in Shandong province with the dubious distinction of having 15 percent of Falun Gong deaths although it has less than 1 percent of China's population. The police repeatedly asked Xuan for money, but his family, being sect practitioners themselves, could not pay the ransom because they had lost their jobs. In retaliation, Xuan was beaten with rubber truncheons and doused in cold water for several hours before he fell into a coma and died.

- Thirty-year-old Chu Congrui, arrested at a protest in Tiananmen Square on December 1, 2000, was reported dead to her family sixteen days later, her face clearly bruised.

- Wang Yijia was practicing Falun Gong exercises in his home in Hengyang, Hunan, in January 2001 when police burst in to arrest him. Refusing to cooperate, Wang ran to the balcony and fell to his death.

- Liu Rongxiu, arrested on December 6, 2000, for protesting in Tiananmen Square, died the following month in a detention center in northern Hebei with bandages around his head and dried blood caked around his mouth.

- Thirty-year-old Liu Jiamin, died on January 7, 2001, from lung injuries after police rammed a tube down her throat to break a hunger strike.

- Thirty-three-year-old Li Mei, died in May 2001 in a "transformation school" in Laiyang, Shandong, after suffering a broken spine and other injuries.

- Thirty-three-year-old Li Changjun, holder of a master's degree, was detained May 16, 2001, after police caught him downloading and printing Falun Gong material from the Internet. He died a week later, his body covered with red bruises and scars, his neck and ears beaten purple.

- Forty-seven-year-old Chen Qiulan, arrested in July 2001 for posting information about the sect on the Internet, died of a heart attack a month later, on August 14, at a detention center in Daqing, Heilongjiang.

- Wu Liangjie, died on August 20, 2001, after falling from a window of a police office in Baicheng, Jilin.

- Thirty-nine-year-old Wang Hong of Liaoning province died on August 31, 2001, after being repeatedly tortured at a labor camp for refusing to renounce her belief in Falun Gong.

- Thirty-three-year-old Chen Aizhong died of respiratory failure on September 20, 2001, at a hospital in Tangshan, Hebei, after suspected force-feeding.

- Thirty-two-year-old Yu Xiuling died on September 19, 2001, after a lengthy beating by the police and being thrown alive from a fourth-story window. Her husband was told that she had leapt to her death.[65]

As if the above cases were not tragic enough, on July 3, 2001, the Hong Kong-based ICHRD said that on June 20, sixteen Falun Gong followers in a labor camp in Harbin attempted mass suicide by hanging themselves with ropes fashioned from bedsheets. Ten of them, all women, died. They were among thirty followers who had gone on a hunger strike, for which they were punished by having their sentences extended by up to six months. Beijing admitted that eleven sect members in the reeducation center had undertaken mass suicide and that three died from the attempt. Foreign ministry spokeswoman Zhang Qiyue said, "This shows once again that Falun Gong is a cult that harms human life." For its part, Falun Gong's office in New York claimed that fifteen followers in that camp were tortured to death.[66]

None of the deaths were reported in the Chinese media; only those directly affected by the crackdown knew of its scope and ferocity. Besides resulting in deaths, Beijing's suppression of Falun Gong had driven people underground, ruined careers, and destroyed families. Two sect adherents who worked in Weifang's city government, for example, were forced to leave their homes to live with relatives out of fear of arrest. Their daughter, also an adherent, was kicked out of her university for refusing to renounce her faith and now drifts from family to family. "This won't go on much longer, will it?" she asked a visitor. "The government has to relent and legalize us. That's all we're asking."[67]

Females seem to be disproportionately represented among sect followers targeted by the government. In part this is due to their being the majority of Falun Gong adherents in China. But there is evidence that Chinese police and officials in work camps also singled out the women for torture. Female practitioners were reportedly subjected to beatings, electric shocks, burnings with cigarette butts or irons and were forced to stand naked in freezing temperatures. At one labor camp in Liaoning province, it was alleged, women were stripped naked and thrown into prison cells with violent male criminals who were encouraged to rape and abuse them. Instead of being punished or reprimanded, the officers in that camp were lauded and were promoted by being assigned to train the staff of other camps. All of which prompted Radhika Coomaraswamy, the United Nation's expert on violence against women, to send a letter of concern to the Chinese government in January 2001.[68]

The Struggle Continues

The Chinese government has vowed it will "fight the war to the end" against Falun Gong. In part, Beijing's ruthless and brutal campaign to exterminate the sect is due to the latter's persistent popularity. Many followers still risk arrest and beatings to perform the exercises, but they do them in their homes instead of public parks.[69]

A Beijing-based analyst maintained that although the Chinese government has succeeded in breaking up the key organizers, it still must deal with "an amorphous movement" for which "the rigid structure of the Communist Party is ill equipped." Under attack, the sect has transformed itself into a nonhierarchical mass movement whose structure mirrors that of the Internet, on which it depends.[70] There are no longer any national Falun Gong posts in China, only local volunteer "tutors" and "facilitators" who look to Master Li for guidance. One such volunteer, Lloyd Zhao　a thirty-three-year-old advanced computer technician—insisted that if he were caught, other devotees would take his place. Until the government succeeded in reeducating or imprisoning every last true believer, he vowed, the network would endure. A senior CCP official wryly observed that the sect was hard to control because its ability to wage guerrilla-style resistance was similar to the underground Communist Party in its years in the wilderness before it eventually succeeded in being the new ruler of China. Professor Lu Xiaobo of Barnard College similarly described Beijing's battle with the sect as "a giant fighting a ghost: you know it is there and haunting you, but you don't exactly know where to attack, or when it will attack you."[71]

More than the sect's elusive but effective organization, the Chinese government is worried about Falun Gong's presence in the armed forces, notwithstanding the reeducation of police and soldiers to shun the sect. To illustrate, in February 2001, a Falun Gong banner flew for nearly an hour at the headquarters of the People's Armed Police in Beijing; supporters also painted slogans inside the tightly guarded air force headquarters in the capital. An internal government estimate had 4,000 to 5,000 sect sympathizers in the 200,000-strong air force.[72]

More than its popularity and organization, the authorities in Beijing are troubled by Falun Gong's similarities to religious movements that had instigated countless uprisings in China's history, some of which toppled entire dynasties. In particular, the sect is remarkably reminiscent of traditional Chinese millenarian movements, sectarian religious societies that anticipate nothing less than the end of days. That history will be the subject of the chapter to follow.

Chapter Two

Chinese Religions and Millenarian Movements

Imperial China is usually thought of as a highly secularized society in which religion held little sway. Such a notion is probably due to the dominance that Confucianism, conventionally understood to be an agnostic philosophy, historically wielded over the Chinese state and society. This view, however, cannot easily be reconciled with the social facts.[1]

To begin with, Confucianism was neither atheistic nor agnostic. Instead, it inherited significant metaphysical elements from the folk religion of Chinese antiquity—heaven, predetermination, divination, and the theory of yin-yang and the five elements. In addition to these supernatural beliefs, Confucianism also mandated the religious practices of ancestor worship and ritualistic sacrifices to heaven.

Nor was Chinese spiritual life composed of only the ancient creed and Confucianism. Although the latter was the official faith of Imperial China, its preeminene was continuously challenged by Daoism and Buddhism. There were also the minor faiths of Islam and Christianity, as well as astrology, chronomancy, and numerous other forms of magic and animism.

In effect, instead of being worldly and secular, traditional China was suffused with sacred practices and beliefs. Religion penetrated every social institution and exerted a profound influence on the people's outlook on life and their daily activities. Today, the temples and shrines that survived the destruction of Mao Zedong's Cultural Revolution still dot the landscape and stand as vivid testament to the pietistic character of old China.[2]

Folk Religion of Antiquity

The folk religion that bequeathed its beliefs and practices to Confucianism was the indigenous faith of the Shang, Zhou, and Early Han dynasties, spanning a period from the dawn of history to A.D. 9.[3] This religion had its roots in Chinese antiquity, a prehistoric time of myth and mysticism. Not unlike other primitive cults, China's folk religion was a pantheistic animism that conceived of nature and the universe as alive, inhabited by gods and spirits.

According to a creation myth from the fourth to the second century B.C., in the beginning there was nothing but a primeval vapor in a shapeless dark expanse, a gaping mass. The effluvium was the embodiment of the cosmic energy *Taiji* (the Great Ultimate) that governed matter, time, and space. At the moment of creation, the misty haze underwent a transformation and differentiated into heaven and earth, male and female, hard and soft matter, and other binary yin-yang phenomena. The interaction of yin and yang produced the building blocks of the universe: the five elements of water, fire, metal, wood, and earth. Their continuous interaction and endless permutations constitute *dao* (the Way), the unity that is the universe.[4]

The supreme governing force in the cosmos was Heaven (*tian* or *tiandi,* the heavenly sovereign-deity). Heaven was more than a governing power; it was a moral force that predetermined the fate of human beings and meted out reward to the virtuous and punishment to the wicked. It was believed that Heaven's plans could be gleaned by shamans through divination and the theory of yin-yang and the five elements.[5]

Yang, the male element, was identified with heaven; the female element yin, with earth. The yang and the yin, by the power of their cooperation, produced all that existed, including human beings, who were shaped out of the same substance that comprised the universe. Being formed of celestial material, human beings were conceived to be intrinsically good, but their benign constitution could be corrupted in the course of life by external influences. Virtue, therefore, required that human beings be carefully guided by instruction and education, and their passions and desires constrained by moral and mental discipline.[6]

It was believed that human beings, being a compound of yang and yin, had two corresponding souls. The first was *shen,* an immaterial soul of yang substance from the ethereal part of the universe, which operated in the living human body as *qi* (breath). A second soul was *gui,* a material soul formed of yin substance which originated from the terrestrial part of the cosmos. When a human being died, her *shen* and *qi* returned to heaven, while her physical body and material soul were restored to the earth.[7]

Being part of the animate cosmos, plants also were believed to have souls. Depending on the amount of soul-substance (*ling*) conferred on them by the universe, certain plants, such as ginseng, were believed to possess great power. Those who consumed such plants could absorb the latter's soul-substance and, consequently, be cured of disease and attain longevity, if not immortality.[8]

More than plants, such objects as the bones of the dead and

wood that had been reduced to stumps, logs, or boards—being part and parcel of the animate universe—were also believed to be alive. Like plants, seemingly inanimate matter also differed in accordance with the amount of soul-substance. Cinnabar, gold, silver, jade, mother-of-pearl, and pearls were believed to be particularly rich in soul-substance and, when ingested, could cure diseases, prolong life, and even revive the moribund.[9]

Confucianism

Elements of this prehistoric cult were retained by Confucianism and Daoism, "twin streams of doctrine" that sprang from the same ancient creed. In the case of Confucianism, its founder, Confucius (551?–479? B.C.), subscribed to the archaic notion that human beings were possessed of dual souls. According to him, upon death the corporeal soul "goes downward" while the ethereal soul "is on high." Like the folk religion, Confucius believed in the original goodness and perfectibility of human nature. He revered tradition and did not claim to bring new ideas, but only to have conformed with the providential order of the universe by preserving the thought of the ancient sages.[10]

The corpus of Confucianism was a prescriptive moral philosophy on right living and virtuous government that placed a high value on order and conformity, tradition and authority. There was an order in the universe that was superior to, but not independent of, human will; the obligation of human beings was to accord themselves to this universal order by regulating their personal conduct and sentiments. As Confucius put it, "From the Son of Heaven to the common people, in the same way, everyone must take as first principle: regulate one's conduct."[11]

Self-regulation demanded that the individual undertake a labor of moral cultivation to become a gentleman (*junzi*). In that endeavor, the individual must strive to acquire and perfect certain virtues, including those of propriety (*li*) and filial piety (*xiao*), and properly observe the five human relations. By becoming a gentleman, an individual would realize the universal order. More than that, if everyone became righteous, a process of moral contagion would spread through wider and wider circles to permeate every individual, family, country, and ultimately the world.[12]

Self-regulation also demanded that human passions be constrained by propriety, rites, and ceremonies (*yi*). The chief rule of life was the golden mean: the practice of moderation to achieve and maintain harmony; excess was regarded to be the gravest of faults. The civilized man should reveal his emotions only through the conventional rules for their expression. By quieting feelings and moderating the expression of joy and grief, rites stripped sentiments of their turbulence and violence. Human passions developed instead in a measured, ordered, and rhythmic fashion. In this manner, the soul would regain its balance for the greater benefit of the self and others, thereby making possible communal life and civilization.[13]

Filial piety was the preeminent principle of moral and religious life. The parent was a stern but benevolent patriarch to whom the child owed unquestioned obedience and devotion. Filial piety was generalized into ancestor worship: it was a public obligation for everyone to honor and pray to the souls of one's forebears who could intercede with Heaven on behalf of the living. Filial piety became the template for all other relations with authority, especially that between emperor and subject.[14] The emperor was to rule with wisdom, charity, and virtue over his children—the people—whose abject obeisance could be abrogated only if the emperor was found to be corrupt or evil. Only then was rebellion justified, because Heaven itself had withdrawn the right to rule from the incumbent ruler.

Rules of propriety also informed the five human relations: those between parent and child, emperor and subject, husband and wife, older and young siblings, and between friends. The first four dyads were unequal authority relationships between a superior and an inferior in which the former enjoyed status, prestige, and power, while the latter's role was to passively obey. A superior was any authority figure, be she or he an emperor, parent, official, landlord, teacher, employer, elder sibling, or any older person, as it was presumed that age was invariably accompanied by wisdom. Only the last human relation—that between friends—was an association between equals where the individual enjoyed a measure of freedom from the rules of propriety. It was this hierarchy of superior-inferior relations that grounded society: each person had an assigned role, the performance and fulfillment of which would assure social order and harmony.

Therein laid the basis of what became China's canonical faith; its influence permeated the entire society. Confucius had lived in a time of social and political turmoil—the Period of the Warring States (771-221 B.C.)—when the feudal system of the Zhou dynasty was breaking down. The dynasty was founded in 1100 B.C., but it had begun to decline in 771 B.C. and was increasingly besieged by nomads from the north. As the power of the Zhou court waned, the nobles in the various domains or states grew increasingly restive. At the same time, new states arose on the dynasty's periphery and absorbed some of the Zhou appanages. As the feudal lords became more independent, they battled each other for dominance—a time of bloody conflict that endured for 550 years, until the warlord of Qin vanquished his rivals and united the feudal estates into a centralized kingdom by 221 B.C.

The teachings of Confucius became the ideological and religious foundation for the new Imperial China that emerged from the chaos. The first emperor of Qin (Qin shihuangdi) abolished feudalism and created in its stead a centralized, bureaucratic empire. In that new China, the emperor was a demigod on whom Heaven had conferred the moral mandate to rule. As the Son of Heaven, the emperor was more than an absolute monarch; he was also the supreme religious leader who mediated between people and Heaven by offering sacrifices to the celestial deity, and he was assisted in his rule by a meritocratic, quasi-sacerdotal class of literati.[15]

Given the turbulent times in which Confucius lived, it should not be surprising that his thought placed a premium on social order and stability. Whatever metaphysical elements Confucius retained from the religion of antiquity seem selected for their functional utility toward the creation and maintenance of a stable and orderly society. The concept of Heaven's mandate provided China's ruler with the necessary political legitimacy. The emphasis on moral perfection meant that instead of relying on a system of laws and regulations, the people would police themselves. The conception of human relations as hierarchical and authoritarian also helped the emperor maintain order and control. Socialized from childhood to obey and submit to the unquestioned authority of parents, the people behaved in like manner toward their political authorities.

For all its emphasis on order and stability, it is ironic that what Confucianism could not provide was an orderly and institionalized method to remove from positions of authority individuals who had abused their power and were wicked instead of virtuous. The supreme ruler, the emperor, could be dislodged only by a massive popular uprising that exacted a great toll in life and property. No wonder, then, that the Chinese historically feared political unrest (*luan*), and their fear in turn led them to yearn for the return of order—even at the expense of personal liberty.

The Chinese believed that loss of Heaven's mandate by an incumbent emperor would be signified by a series of ominous signs that included such climactic disturbances as earthquakes, floods, and comets; degeneration of the hydraulic system of river dikes and irrigation canals, resulting in poor harvests; political corruption; and increasing rural unrest. Given these traditional beliefs, when a series of natural disasters occurred, the people understood them as signs of Heaven's displeasure with the reigning emperor. Convinced of the dynasty's loss of the mandate to rule, the masses would rise up in rebellion (*geming*, literally, to withdraw the mandate). Indeed, it has been observed that no country has a richer or more lengthy legacy of peasant revolts than China.[16]

As Confucianism became institutionalized, its teachings became routine and ritualistic. In the place of personal cultivation was an increasingly formalist subjection to tradition and custom. The tales of filial piety that had instructed and inspired took on a stiff and exaggerated aspect. In the course of time, Confucianism devolved into an ideology of moral positivism based simply on social conformity.[17]

Daoism

Like Confucianism, Daoism also inherited from China's ancient cult. Unlike Confucianism, however, Daoism was more heavily steeped in mysticism—in the traditional secrets of spells and talismans; of rules of divination and magical prayers; and of astral, medical, and pharmaceutical science. One of those secrets was qigong: the use of breathing exercises to prolong the retention of air, a practice that was believed to increase potency and longevity. These mystical practices of antiquity had been largely abandoned by the Confucian literati as they became increasingly preoccupied with ethics and morality.[18]

Being more mystical, Daoism became the natural refuge for the popular customs and traditions that official Confucianism had banished from society. The Daoist pantheon embraced a host of deities in charge of points in the human life cycle and aspects of nature, including divinities of grottoes, springs, abysses, and peaks. The gods and spirits were arranged in a hierarchy paralleling that of the imperial bureaucracy. The latter ruled the secular world, while a divine administration was in charge of the afterlife. After the seventh century, cross-pollination from Buddhism led to the Daoist belief in a posthumous retribution for human actions. A code was elaborated that assigned precise values to sins and to compensatory virtuous behavior.[19]

Daoism also differed in its approach to the vicissitudes of life. Eschewing Confucianism's preoccupation with human relations, the Daoists recommended instead the detachment of the self, emotionally if not physically, from human intercourse and society. All values were artificial: one should prize neither oneself, nor honors, nor friends, masters, and kin. Even life itself was unimportant, for what was life but an illusion? In the words of the Daoist philosopher Zhuangzi: "Am I a man dreaming that I am a butterfly, or am I rather a butterfly dreaming that it is a man?"

The aim of religious life was the Way (*dao*), the ecstasy that came from melding oneself with the universe. To achieve that union, an ascetic way of life was necessary, as well as a systematic inertia (*wuwei*) whereby control was achieved, paradoxically, by letting things go. Reason was suspect; true wisdom consisted in emptying one's heart and mind of every idea and sentiment. The sage lived in retreat by avoiding all human attachments—those of love, lust, fame, fortune, popularity, and success. Bending and yielding before everything, like water, the sage allowed himself to drift.[20]

The literature of Daoism is immense. Most of the mystical works of Daoism seemed to be the product of revelation and were neither dated nor signed. The philosophical Daoist tracts were identified with Laozi (*Daode jing*), Zhuangzi, and Liehzi who lived in the fourth and third centuries B.C. After its beginning, Daoism rapidly spread through China and became a popular religion by sectarian movements. The first Daoist communities were formed in Shandong and Sichuan. By the middle of the eighth century, there were more than 1,600 Daoist temples staffed by priests and nuns across China. In A.D. 1113, a hierarchy of Daoist prelates was established and recognized by the state.[21]

Buddhism

The only one of Imperial China's three major religions that was not indigenous, Buddhism made its way from India into China under the Han dynasty (206 B.C.-A.D. 25). After quite arduous beginnings, the imported faith took nearly five centuries to establish itself firmly in China but became quite popular under the Tang and Song dynasties.[22]

Perhaps it was no accident that Daoism and Buddhism were the main religious rivals of Confucianism. The latter emphasized propriety and conformity and was chiefly concerned with the temporal world of human relations, a preoccupation that could become stifling for the individual. The appeal of Confucianism's rivals, therefore, was precisely their otherworldly orientation, their insistence that life was ephemeral and that the pain and vexation that are part and parcel of human existence could be transcended through emotional and physical detachment.

In the case of Buddhism, the aim of religious life was enlightenment through meditation. Outside the inner life, all was vain and impermanent—mere illusions and mirages. Human life was as evanescent as morning dew or raindrops falling in water. Wisdom (*bodhi*) was the result not of reason, but of an intuition of the heart, the condition for which was a state of peace and repose. Once that thought was comprehended, salvation was achieved; from then there would be neither life nor death nor the endless chain of rebirth.[23]

Souls transmigrated at death and were reincarnated anew as a human being, animal, demon, or god. The transmigration was governed by a moral law (*karma*) that was the result of the sum of good and bad actions committed during previous existences. Rebirth in an unpleasant form could be avoided by practicing charity (*paramita*) and avoiding sin, such as killing, stealing, usury, adultery, deceit, cursing, eating meat, smoking, and imbibing alcohol.[24]

Even better than a good reincarnation was not to be reborn at all, to be liberated from the karmic wheel. Those who achieved enlightenment and were freed from the cycle of reincarnation and rebirth became buddhas; those who had attained nirvana but chose to return in human form to save humanity were bodhisattvas. In effect, every human being could attain divinity. Together, buddhas and bodhisattvas formed a numberless pantheon of gods in the Buddhist theogony.

As the defenders of national traditions, the Confucian literati kept careful watch over both Daoism and Buddhism. In particular, the latter's monastic institutions—whereby men and women renounced society to become celibate monks and nuns—posed a threat to the Confucian social order founded on filial piety and ancestor worship. It was for that reason that Buddhism was periodically subjected to violent persecution, as in A.D. 444, 626, and 845. But despite these pogroms, Buddhism endured and was not significantly weakened.[25]

In this manner, orthodox Confucianism and its Buddhist and Daoist religious rivals managed to coexist through the ages. The effect of this religious cohabitation was to increase the people's indifference to dogma, along with the number of gods. In the place of doctrinairism was a syncretic pragmatism: the Chinese people accepted and made use of all religious formulas to the extent that they showed themselves to be effective, convinced that each religion and god might be good for some purpose, at a given moment, in a special case, or for a particular individual.[26]

Religion and State in Traditional China

In spite of the existence of other faiths, Confucianism claimed for itself a predominant role as the reigning orthodoxy because it was more than a religion; it was Imperial China's state ideology. In this regard, there is a marked difference between China and the experience of Western Europe. Although the Catholic Church wielded considerable power over the European monarchies, church and state were never completely united. As a result, both church and state had to continuously contend with each other, resulting in the circumscribing, rather than the maximization, of their respective power.

From its beginning, the Catholic Church struggled to exert its spiritual and temporal power over the monarchs of Europe—a struggle that became increasingly difficult beginning in the sixteenth century when Rome found its authority challenged by the Protestant Reformation. The Vatican's power was further eroded in the eighteenth century by a new philosophical movement that emphasized human beings' capacity to reason. This was the Enlightenment that eventually led to the scientific revolution, democratic government, and the formal separation of church and state in Western Europe.

For their part, the European monarchs' power, though autocratic, was not absolute because they had to grapple with the Church in Rome. As an example, witness the struggle between the English Crown and the Vatican, a struggle that became acute during the reigns of King Henry II (vs. Thomas Beckett) and Henry VIII. The latter eventually succeeded in freeing the English monarchy from

Rome's dictates by establishing an independent (Anglican) Church of England.

In contrast, religion and state were fused in Imperial China from its beginning. More than being commingled, religion sanctioned the state, as the entire political legitimacy of Imperial China was founded on the Confucian precept of the mandate of Heaven. The fusion of church and state in Imperial China not only conferred preeminent status to Confucianism, it also vastly inflated the power of the state. Being both temporal head of state and religious leader of the (Confucian) church, the Chinese emperor's power was total and absolute, unchecked by man or institution.[27] For that power to remain thus, however, such voluntary groups as guilds and clan associations as well as China's other religions had to be brought under state control because they posed nothing less than a cosmological challenge to the power of the emperor as Son of Heaven.[28] Religions that were organized and financed by tithes from a mass following constituted a particular threat. Being organized, such religions carried the potential of being a competitive center of power should their leaders become politically ambitious.

As the official faith, Confucianism jealously guarded its perquisites by subordinating its rivals and relegating them to the status of "heterodoxy" (*yiduan*, literally, "strange principles" or "heresy"). Not only did the other faiths have to obtain official permission by registering with the state, restrictions were imposed on their activities.[29] As an example, finding his authority threatened by charismatic preachers and mystics, an emperor during the Ming dynasty (1368–1644) sought to control religion by issuing the following decree: "Religious leaders . . . who hold meetings which take place late at night and break up by day, whereby the people are stirred up and misled under the pretext of cultivating virtue, shall be sentenced, the principal perpetrators to strangulation, and their accomplices to a hundred blows with the long stick, followed by a lifelong banishment to a distance of three thousand *li*."[30]

In effect, the Chinese government historically regarded all non-Confucian faiths as more than religious rivals—they were seen as incipient political competitors, each carrying the seed of rebellion. This meant that religious groups that could not obtain official sanction or refused to submit to state control were driven underground to operate furtively as secret societies. Their secrecy, in turn, provoked the state's suspicion and persecution. Persecution, in turn, politicized erstwhile apolitical religious groups, their very politicization only confirming the government's original suspicions. In this manner, by its religious intolerance, the Chinese state created its own nemesis. Today, facing what they see as a similar threat from Falun Gong, China's political leaders have responded in like fashion.

Although dynastic rule in China nominally ended in 1911, there are significant continuities between the People's Republic of China and its imperial predecessor. In past and present China, the penetration of state power ends at the county level, leaving the villages to substantial self-rule.[31] In Imperial China, the state maintained extensive trade monopolies over salt, iron, tea, wines, and spirits; in the PRC today, inefficient state-owned enterprises still hobble economic productivity. In the past as well as today, the upper stratum of Chinese society is composed of an overlapping political-economic elite: Imperial China's mandarins, gentry, and landlords, and today's party-government-big business elites. Today, as in the past, "the tentacles of the state Moloch" still try to superintend in detail the actions of people from the cradle to the grave.[32]

Last but not the least, in both past and present China, church and state are commingled. Since its inception in 1949, the PRC was and remains an ideocracy: a political system where the right to rule is based on the government's claim to possess special truths and insights imparted by an absolutist and comprehensive ideology.[33] In the case of contemporary China, despite the bankruptcy of Marxism-Leninism, the Chinese Communist Party continues to justify its rule with its variant of Marxist ideology that presumes to know the past and present as well as to predict the course of societal evolution. It is this ideology that allegedly endows the party with the special knowledge and insight to govern China as its vanguard.

At the same time, and especially after the 1989 pro-democracy movement that was suppressed only after the government called on the People's Liberation Army to wield its deadly force against unarmed civilians, the Communist Party is increasingly turning to patriotic nationalism to supplement the official Marxist ideology.[34] In effect, whatever its content, ideology in the People's Republic functions as a religion by eliciting the same faith, fervor of commitment, and resistance to empirical confirmation as religion. Like the emperors of old, the Communist Party justifies its monopoly on political power through recourse to religion, albeit the secular faith of a political ideology. And, as in the past, the fusion of church and state has resulted in a Leviathan state unchecked by man or institution.

Secret Societies and Millenarian Movements

In Imperial China, despite the government's strictures, powerful religious movements still managed, from time to time, to challenge the supremacy of Confucianism. Not having official sanction, these movements were labeled "cults" (*xiejiao*).[35] Typically they were syncretic sects of Buddhism and Daoism. These sectarian religious movements were instrumental in fomenting popular rebellions and dynastic changes in Chinese history.

Those religious movements invariably took the form of secret societies: informal popular institutions created by marginalized men seeking mutual aid and protection in a hazardous world. As such, they were a type of brotherhood association, similar to the burial or "father and mother" society in traditional China and the *tong* of North American Chinatowns. Like other fraternal associations, secret societies served as a substitute lineage for those who had lost their family or village affiliations. Calling each other brothers, the members afforded a measure of social security when no other existed, providing succor and support in sickness, disaster, or death. Although peasants comprised the majority of secret society membership, there were adherents from the lower scholar-gentry class who shared the same political and social objectives.[36]

It was those goals that mainly distinguished secret societies from other self-help groups. More than providing mutual assistance, secret societies were voluntary autonomous associations in conscious opposition to oppression by the state or by the wealthy and powerful gentry-landowning elite. During the Yuan (1280–1368) and Qing (1644–1912) dynasties, when China was ruled by the ethnically alien Mongols and Manchus, respectively, secret societies were also protonationalist movements intent on overthrowing the government, not simply because it was oppressive, but because it was controlled by non-Han Chinese.[37]

Secret societies also differed from other fraternal associations in their employment of esoteric symbols and rituals drawn from the realms of popular religion. Symbols typically included charms and amulets believed to protect users from danger; rituals included initiation rites of blood oaths and ordeal. The religious symbols and rituals supplemented the secular safety net of mutual aid by conferring supernatural protection on the members. From the state's perspective, however, the inclusion of beliefs, symbols, and rituals from "heterodox" cults made the secret societies more than illegal—they represented nothing less than a challenge to the Confucian state-religion that legitimated the emperor's rule.[38]

Some secret societies adopted more than symbols and rituals

from popular religions; they were also millenarian. The word "millenarian" comes from Christianity and refers to the conviction that Christ the Lord will come again to create a kingdom on earth and, with the assistance of a select chosen people, reign over it for a thousand years before the Final Judgment.

Its meaning broadened to include secular movements, "millenarian" also refers to "powerfully emotional social movements whose members anticipate a unique type of social salvationism" whereby the complete destruction of the existing order would herald the arrival of a new and perfect society. Victory, believed to be inevitable and according to divine plan, would be the final denouement of history. As used in its secular sense, it can be argued that all political revolutions are millenarian in varying degrees and forms. In the West there is a long tradition of such movements, including the Hebrew Maccadeban revolt ca. 165 B.C.; medieval West European peasant movements, such as the Taborites of Bohemia, the League of the Elect, and the Anabaptists; and the Nazi, fascist, and communist revolutions that so defined the twentieth century.[39]

There are some who reject the conception of millenarian movements as outbursts of psychopathological behavior, arguing instead that they are "revitalization movements"—instruments of social renewal. According to this view, when a society is suffering severe collective stress and potential cultural disintegration, some in the community recognize, long before most other people, that the continuation of their way of life is in peril and that the end of what now exists may be near.[40] They become convinced that only a new and potent ideology can save society. That renaissance, however, requires the total elimination of the existing society. Only then can the world be made anew with the dawning of a nascent epoch of peace and prosperity—the secular analogue to Christ's Second Coming. In effect, it is argued, far from being symptomatic of collective psychopathy, millenarian movements should be understood as prescient and rational responses to great social distress.

Three conditions that give rise to millenarian movements have been identified.[41] The first is collective psychohistorical dislocation: mass trauma, stress, and disorientation experienced by a populace as a result of great social upheavals, such as colonialism, imperialism, rapid industrialization and modernization, natural disasters, and political-social oppression.[42] The people react to their distress with moral outrage and righteous indignation, articulated as collective demands for justice. When the demands are mishandled by the political authorities, political violence erupts.

A second condition for millenarian movements is a religious tradition of apocalyptic messianism. When a society with such a heritage finds itself in the throes of massive social dislocation, its populace is inclined to understand and to seek remedy for its distress with the language of religious messianism. People anticipate that the end days are imminent, a time when a savior will appear to sweep away the corruption of the extant society. If a charismatic leader then emerges to articulate popular disaffection and sound the clarion call for social revitalization—all in the nomenclature of religious messianism—the third and final condition for the instigation of a millenarian movement will have been met.

Chinese Millenarian Movements

Like their counterparts in Europe and elsewhere, Chinese secret societies were mutual-aid associations at odds with the reigning power structure. More than that, secret societies were directly involved in all of the peasant rebellions in Chinese history. Even in times of peace, the societies acted as agents of continuity by sustaining political and social opposition against the regime.[43]

In theory, there were two types of Chinese secret societies: secular political groups opposed to the ruling dynasty, and sectarian religious societies that were Buddhist/Daoist and, in some instances, Manichean in inspiration. In many cases, however, groups that began as religious societies later became politicized. The transmutation of formerly apolitical faith-based groups into stridently political movements renders the analytical demarcation between political and religious secret societies less than clear in practice.

Historically, the appearance of religious movements and other secret societies in China tended to coincide with the end of dynasties, beginning with the first recorded case of a rebellion undertaken by a secret society in 209 B.C. against the Qin dynasty. Like the founder of Falun Gong, the leaders of that ancient rebellion—Chen Sheng and Wu Guang—had espoused beliefs of a spiritual nature.

Northern China was particularly prone to the rise of religious secret societies, many of which were animated by millenarian and utopian aspirations. This was probably due to the region's harsh climate and inhospitable terrain, which made the lives of its inhabitants particularly challenging, prompting them to seek consolation in the supernatural. The most famous Daoist sectarian movement was that of the Yellow Turbans who revolted in A.D. 184, believing that their leader, Zhang Jue, was the promised savior. Although unsuccessful at the time, their revolt, together with the rebellion of the Five Bushels of Rice Society twelve years later, helped bring down the second Han dynasty. The Yellow Turbans were influenced by primarily Daoist doctrine and language, as were many other rebellions during the next 250 years. Other religious societies were Buddhist in inspiration in that they anticipated the imminent arrival of messianic buddhas who would lead humankind to paradise. One of the earliest was the Mahayana Rebellion in A.D. 515 led by Buddhist clerics who were convinced that a new epoch had arrived in China.[44]

The White Lotus Society

The most important Buddhist secret society was that of the White Lotus, a sectarian movement that was instrumental in overthrowing the Yuan dynasty. Some historians maintain that despite their different names, northern China's religious secret societies were in fact "all part of one long-lived cleverly camouflaged cabal" called the White Lotus. The latter was not a monolithic organization but instead was made up of small scattered groups of believers in a common religion transmitted down the centuries via long and loose chains of teachers and disciples. As one scholar put it, "There was . . . no single 'White Lotus Society.' There was only a diverse White Lotus religious teaching that found expression in sects calling themselves by a wide variety of names."[45] Because of the similarities of beliefs between Falun Gong and the White Lotus, the latter's ideology merits some special attention.

The White Lotus began to be active around A.D. 1360. The roots of its religious beliefs, however, reached back into Chinese antiquity. The central deity of the White Lotus was a creator goddess named Wusheng laomu (Unbegotten Eternal Mother) who was associated with millenial expectations as early as the first century B.C. The great goddess was known by other names, including Wusheng fumu (Unbegotten Progenitor), Wusheng fomu (Unbegotten Buddha Mother), Yaochi jinmu (Golden Mother of the Jade Pool), and Laoshengmu (Venerable Sagely Mother).[46] By whatever name, she was believed to be the progenitor of humanity when she gave birth to a son and daughter who married and, in turn, gave birth to humans. The newly created men and women were sent by the great goddess to live on earth in the nirvana of the "Eastern world." But their stay in paradise was short-lived as they soon "indulged in vanity and lost their original nature." As a result of their Fall, all living things "were confused and lost in the red dust world; they had fallen and knew not how to return to their origin." Longing and weeping for her children, the mother goddess urged them to forsake avarice and "the world of true emptiness" to return to their primordial land—their "original home" where "birth and death forever cease." There, mother and children would reunite and sit together in bliss on the golden lotus.[47]

To save humanity, the great goddess would send buddhas down to earth to teach a salvific morality to her wayward children. Human beings being "steeped in wickedness," however, their salvation required repeated efforts. She sent down, in succession, the Lamp-Lighting Buddha (Randengfo) and Sakyamuni Buddha (Shijiafo). Alas, each could save only some of her children, leaving most of humanity still benighted. The salvation of the remainder would be undertaken by a third and last god, Buddha Maitreya (Milefo).[48]

The arrival of each buddha was believed to coincide with the end of a historical era called *kalpa* (*jieshu*). Traditional Buddhist thought conceived of history as divided into great periods, each lasting hundreds of thousands of years. Each era would steadily degenerate, at the end of which Buddhist teachings would appear, initially prevail, but gradually become undermined. In the end, a holocaust would destroy the world and a new *kalpa* would begin. White Lotus sects believed there would be only three *kalpa,* lasting 108,000, 27,000, and 97,200 years, respectively. The end of each *kalpa* would be marked by great disorder brought about by human wickedness and natural disasters—"the five grains will not grow" and the people will be in great distress. The calamities were sent down by the Great Mother to punish humankind for refusing salvation and forsaking the true way. The apocalypse would be signaled by a black wind of destruction that would sweep the world for seven days and seven nights. At the end of each *kalpa,* the men and women who were saved would be greeted by a Dragon Flower Assembly (*longhua hui*) held in the mother goddess' palace and attended by all the gods and immortals.[49]

The White Lotus Society believed that humanity, despite its lack of recollection or historical documentation, had already experienced two epochs and was in the third great *kalpa*, which would end when the Great Mother dispatch the third buddha to save the faithful. The exact timing of the end days would be signified by two events. The first was a series of great calamities, followed by the second event—the appearance of the third buddha. Thus it was that in the course of Chinese history, when there had been a succession of natural disasters, believers began looking for Buddha Maitreya. In such a time, a charismatic man claiming to be Buddha and proselytizing a new faith might gain a large following. The buddha incarnate was believed to have no special identifying physical trait or behavior other than a generally extraordinary appearance and a surname of Li, Liu, Zhu, Zhang, or Wang.[50] When the self-proclaimed Buddha Maitreya determined that the millennium was imminent, his believers would cast aside their private devotions to become openly defiant rebels against the state and the established order.

Primarily a religious body, the White Lotus nevertheless became restive as a result of religious persecution and political disaffection. This pattern of initially religious groups becoming politicized was widespread and characterized a myriad of subsequent secret societies that included the Triads (alleged by some to be the successor to the White Lotus), Nien, Red Spears, Big Swords, Small Daggers, Yellow Beards, Eight Trigrams (another offshoot of the White Lotus), the Society of the Faith, and the Boxers.[51]

The Eight Trigrams

Religious movements and other secret societies were particularly prolific during China's last dynasty. One account maintains that secret societies began to proliferate only during the eighteenth century, being relatively rare in pre-Qing China. A factor that accounted for their abundance in the Qing dynasty was demographic explosion—the population of China nearly doubled in a century, from 150 million in 1650 to 270 million by 1776.[52]

A major millenarian movement in the Qing dynasty was that of the Eight Trigrams, a 300-year-old offshoot of the White Lotus Society. The Eight Trigrams began as a loose and uncoordinated collection of nonviolent Buddhist sects. Convinced by prophecies in their sacred literature that the destruction of the existing society and the arrival of the third and last buddha were imminent, the sects joined together to overthrow the government and, in so doing, bring about the anticipated apocalypse. It was believed that in the coming end days, only those who had joined the Eight Trigrams would live; all others would perish in the chaos.[53]

Despite the watchful eye of the government, the Eight Trigrams managed to rally more than 100,000 people to their cause through a system of personal networks of recruitment and organization. On October 8, 1813, more than a hundred peasant members of the Eight Trigrams gathered outside the Forbidden City in Beijing to seize the imperial palace, convinced that the masses would join them in rebellion. At the same time, insurrections were launched in a dozen cities in three provinces. But the attempt to seize the palace was quickly thwarted, and government troops were dispatched to restore order in the provinces. The rebels eventually were besieged in a city in northern Honan province, and after three days of fighting, the rebellion of the Eight Trigrams was brought to an end. Although the insurrection failed, it exacted a toll of nearly 80,000 lives.[54]

The Taiping Rebellion

Given traditional China's stratified class system, it is not surprising that many secret societies, religious or secular, were fueled by a desire for utopian egalitarianism. As an example, Li Zicheng, the leader of the rebellion that eventually toppled the Ming dynasty, had founded a primitive yet practical egalitarian and utopian state in northwest China in 1643. In 1850, thirty-seven years after the failed insurrection of the Eight Trigrams, Imperial China was again convulsed by an uprising with communal and millenarian aspirations. This was the Taiping Rebellion of 1850 to 1864.

The conditions that gave rise to the rebellion stemmed from China's defeat by the British in the Opium War (1840–42). Not only did the war corrode the legitimacy of the Qing dynasty; the indemnities imposed on the Chinese government were passed on to the common folk as increasingly onerous taxation. At the same time, the defeat pried China open to missionary activities and foreign trade, especially Western imports that greatly affected native industries. All of which resulted in cultural and economic dislocation for the Chinese masses. Exacerbating the popular sense of distress was a continuing population explosion and the resultant agrarian crisis: between 1772 and 1812, China's population grew by 190 percent, while its cultivated lands increased only 35 percent. As one account described it, "By the middle of the century, there was simply not enough food available. Famine became epidemic." In addition, there was a series of natural disasters in the 1840s—the traditional harbingers of a dynasty's loss of the mandate of Heaven. Repeated breaks in the dikes of the Yellow River, the flooding of the lower Yangzi River, drought, storms, and infestation devastated crops and took millions of lives. In the midst of this chaos, all that was needed was a charismatic leader who could articulate popular discontent into a call to revolution.[55]

That individual was Hong Xiuquan, a frustrated aspirant to the mandarin elite who twice failed the imperial civil service examination. Hong devised an eclectic ideology, combining elements of traditional dynastic uprisings with radical new ideas. Under the veneer of a banal and superficial Christianity inspired by a pamphlet he received from a missionary, Hong created an ideological stew comprised of anti-Manchu nationalism, an incipient economic developmental plan, communism, asceticism, gender and class egalitarianism, and a political system of elected officials led by an aristocratic elite with Hong, the Heavenly Prince, at its pinnacle.

With the objective of creating a Heavenly Kingdom of Peace (*taiping tianguo*) on earth, the Taiping Rebellion erupted in 1850. The rebels included poverty-stricken peasants, jobless coolie porters, opium smugglers, pirates, and anti-Manchu secret society members loyal to the Ming dynasty. Beginning in the mountains of Guangxi, the rebels advanced rapidly northward. Three years later, they declared the instauration of a new kingdom at Nanjing. For fourteen years the greatest revolution of the nineteenth-century world engulfed half of China's provinces, laid waste to 600 cities, and took some 20 million lives. Only with the greatest of effort was the rebellion suppressed with ethnic Chinese provincial armies and a small contingent of Western mercenaries, aided by the Taipings' own dissolution into internal rivalry and corruption. Hong committed suicide and his followers either fled, were captured, or were killed by the government.

The Boxers

With the Taiping Rebellion suppressed, the dynasty was preserved, but China arguably was worse off than before. As the rebellion was raging, China suffered a second defeat at the hands of the British (the Second Anglo-Chinese War of 1857–60). That debacle was followed, in 1895, by an even more humiliating drubbing by the Japanese in the war of 1894–95. From there China rapidly descended into disarray. In 1898, a last-gasp effort at reform by constitutional monarchists around young Emperor Guangxu (1875–1908) was sabotaged by the aged Dowager Empress Cixi and court conservatives.

By the beginning of the twentieth century, not only had China lost all its vassal states, it had ceded to the various imperialist powers Macao, Hong Kong, Taiwan, and the Penghu Islands; leased off Kowloon, New Territories, Jiazhou Bay, Lushun, Dalian, Weihaiwei, and Guangzhou Bay; opened eighty-two coastal and inland ports to foreign trade; and marked off areas in sixteen cities as foreign concessions. Through their spheres of influence, the Western powers and Japan enjoyed all the privileges and perquisites of colonizers without any of the attendant obligations and responsibilities, setting up instead "a many-tiered structure of exploitation to fleece the Chinese people."[56]

That exploitation, along with the treaty ports along the coast and the Yangzi River, made the lives of the masses increasingly difficult, so much so that far more Chinese than ever before were struggling for bare existence. As one account put it, "The common people are impoverished, have no one to appeal to, and are as oppressed as if they were hanging upside down." In 1900, the immiseration of the masses erupted in xenophobic violence against Westerners, particularly Christian missionaries and their Chinese converts.[57]

The Boxers (*Yiho quan:* Righteous and Harmonious Fists) began as a peasant secret society that was probably an offshoot of the White Lotus system. Originating in northern China's Zhili and Shandong provinces, the Boxers were a millenarian sect that employed charms and amulets to render believers invulnerable to danger. Those northern provinces had endured natural disasters, as well as cultural and economic dislocation brought about by foreign imports and missionary activities. Convinced that their suffering portended the end times, the Boxers announced in 1899 that a series of catastrophes, the "ten calamities," was imminent and would be immediately followed by social salvation.[58] Beginning in Shandong, with the covert support and encouragement of xenophobic forces in the Qing court, the Boxers rapidly advanced upon the capital, setting fire to churches and the British legation and killing

Christians and foreign diplomats. By mid-June 1900, Beijing and Tianjin were under assault.

In response, the Great Powers dispatched an allied force of 2,100 troops that succeeded in suppressing the popular movement. Beijing was sacked and a severely punitive settlement forced upon the Chinese government. The Boxer Protocol of September 1901 demanded the emperor's apology and expiation, banned the importation of arms and ammunition into China for five years, razed all forts from Beijing to the coast, and required that China pay an indemnity of 67 million pounds, the amortization of which—together with accrued interest—came to 20 million pounds a year. Until the indemnity was fully paid, the Powers would hold as collateral China's maritime and internal customs, together with the revenue generated from its lucrative salt tax. To pay its debt, the Chinese government sought recourse to usurious taxation: new taxes were piled on old under a variety of names, promoting corruption by provincial and local officials who increased taxes at every level until they were ten or more times what the government itself had authorized.[59]

Conclusion

These conditions convinced Chinese intellectuals to turn to revolution as a solution. They began in 1911 with the Republican revolution that overthrew dynastic rule and, with that, Imperial China. Instigated by Sun Yat-sen's Revolutionary Party (*gemindang*, later renamed *guomindang* or Nationalist Party), the revolutionaries were aided by the Triads and the Elder Brothers secret societies who shared the revolutionaries' social and ideological convictions and collaborated with them on political and military issues. More than that, the secret societies organized and led peasant rebellions that substantially contributed to the dynasty's collapse.[60]

But the revolution of 1911 failed at instituting a stable and effective government. In 1949, after a protracted struggle, the Chinese Communist Party routed the Nationalists from the mainland to the island redoubt of Taiwan. Secret societies also played a role in the Chinese Communist revolution. Many early leaders of the CCP, such as Zhu De, He Long, and Liu Zitan, were erstwhile members of secret societies who later exploited their connections to further their party's interests.[61] More important, in their early years, the Chinese Communists experienced little success until Mao Zedong reminded them of the latent power of the peasants and their historical role in fomenting rebellions. It was only then that the CCP transferred its focus from the urban workers to the peasantry and began mobilizing the latter with a utopian ideology of Marxist communism. In effect, since 209 B.C. when the first rebellion by a secret society overthrew the Qin dynasty, millenarian movements had exerted a profound impact on the course of Chinese history. For that matter, the last millenarian movement that succeeded in overthrowing the state was none other than the Communist revolution of 1949.

In January 2001, commenting on Beijing's ruthless crackdown on what it calls the Falun Gong cult, the *Economist* wryly observed, "It takes a cult to know a cult."[62] Having come to power by exploiting China's millenarian tradition, the Communist Party is only too mindful of the potency of such movements. This could explain why party leaders reacted with such alarm and urgency to the peaceful demonstration on April 25, 1999, of more than 10,000 followers of a new religious sect called Falun Gong.

The leadership of Falun Gong has insisted that the sect is not a religion but merely promotes spiritual and moral cultivation. An examination of its belief system, however, indicates otherwise. Not only are the sect's beliefs Buddhist in inspiration, they also draw from Daoism as well as the folk religion of antiquity, especially the practice of qigong. More important, the sect is apocalyptic and millenarian.[63]

Chapter Three
Falun Gong: Beliefs and Practices

Given China's long history of religious persecution, it would be prudent for Falun Gong to eschew identifying itself as a religion. Indeed, its founder and master, Li Hongzhi, is insistent that his teachings constitute a "cultivation practice" (*xiulian*) rather than a religion (*zongjiao*). Likewise, his disciples are vehement that Falun Dafa is not a religion, but instead fosters the cultivation of "moral qualities."[1]

Li maintains that although Falun Gong has certain characteristics in common with religion—those of "cultivation" and "salvation"—it does not qualify as a religion because it lacks "form" (*xingshi*).[2] By that he seems to be referring to *organized* religion with a hierarchy of authority and a professional clergy, individuals whose vocation is religious worship and service. In contrast, Falun Gong is loosely organized at best and does not have a clerical corps; its followers remain "ordinary people" (*changren*) fully engaged in society.

Although rejecting the appellation of religion, Li has hinted that there might come a time when Falun Gong would become organized. Responding to a question posed by one of the sect's guidance counselors in a seminar on September 18, 1994, he allowed that "in the future, we will have disciples who specialize in cultivation, but now we have not yet taken this step." On another occasion, Li said that a nonprofit Falun Dafa Foundation would be instituted sometime in the future, managed by "professional disciples" (*zhuanxiu dizi*) and "monks" (*chujia ren*). In so saying, he seemed to anticipate that at some unspecified future time, his sect would mature into a full-fledged organized faith.[3]

In spite of Falun Gong's somewhat disingenuous claim that it is merely a "cultivation practice," it can be considered a religion if by religion one means a set of metaphysical convictions that include supernatural beings and an afterlife. More than being a religion, an examination of Falun Gong's beliefs and practices, as revealed in Li's writings and lectures, indicates that it bears striking similarities to such historical Chinese sectarian religious societies as the White Lotus and the Eight Trigrams. Although Li disavows a belief in the main deity of those two societies—the Unbegotten Eternal Mother (*Wusheng laomu*)—his ideas are similar to theirs in the eclectic blending of Buddhism, Daoism, classical folk religion, and magic.[4] To this amalgam are added some modern touches: just as the ideology of the Taiping rebels was modernized by a banal Christianity, the beliefs of Falun Gong are given a contemporary veneer via references to science and UFOs.

Cosmology

There is no best place to begin to outline the belief system of Falun Gong, but a logical point of beginning may be an analysis of its cosmology. Li Hongzhi, however, has warned his followers that the cosmos is "simply too profound and mysterious."[5] It is at least that. If anything, his characterization of the cosmos leaves one more confused than illuminated and more perplexed than reassured. In part, this is due to his propensity of using the word "universe" to refer to different celestial entities.

The "universe" (*yuzhou*) we know, according to Li, is but one of countless universes, all of which make up an inclusive mega-cosmos too immense "to describe it in human language." Our "little universe," like all the other universes, contains billions of galaxies bordered by an outer "shell." Some three thousand such universes comprise a "layer" (*ceng*) of a composite mega-universe. Ten thousand to a hundred million layers, in turn, constitute a layer of "celestial body" (*tianti*). Altogether, Li informs us, there are more than eighty-one layers of celestial bodies containing universes so numerous that they "can't be counted with human numbers."[6]

Li compares the intricate structure of the cosmos to the relation between elementary particles: "It is like small particles making up atomic nuclei, atomic nuclei making up atoms, atoms making up molecules." At the extreme edge of the mega-cosmos, there is "complete emptiness where nothing exists." Any matter or object that enters into that void will instantly disintegrate. Further beyond this emptiness, however, is an even larger celestial body where matter, life, space, and time are entirely different. That large and singular celestial body is made up of deities—of "Buddhas, Taos [Daos], and Gods [*shen*]."[7]

The complex structure of the mega-cosmos apparently is duplicated in microcosms of worlds within worlds. As Li describes it: "One grain of sand contains three thousand worlds . . . [with] Buddhas, Taos, and Gods as well as human beings, animals, substances, mountains, water, heaven, earth, air. . . . . The human beings inside grains of sand are just like us. The skin color varies from black, to white, to yellow. . . . If you could see, you would find on your body hair many cities, where trains and cars are running." Inside the worlds contained within a grain of sand are "more microscopic and still more microscopic worlds," each of which contains even more minuscule grains of sand that, in turn, contain three thousand more microscopic worlds containing still more microscopic grains of sand—and so on to infinity.[8]

In these universes within universes, there are multiple dimensions and many "vertical levels." As Li put it, "as soon as you were born, you were also born simultaneously in many dimensions of the universe. They consist of an integrated entity with you, and they are all related and connected mentally." Our bodies in the other dimensions, according to Li, resemble us, except that they are stronger, more beautiful, and "float" (*piao*) instead of walk. They are also our moral superiors, being desirous of neither fame nor fortune. Human beings as well as other life-forms, however, are not cognizant of their corresponding selves in the other dimensions because one "can only know what is in its dimension and will not know anything beyond its dimension." When human beings die, only the bodies in "this material dimension of ours" cease to exist; their bodies in other dimensions still live. If all of this seems abstruse, it is not surprising. Li himself admitted that this phenomenon of multiple dimensions "is extremely complicated."[9]

Gods

In the vast and expansive cosmos, as Li conceived it, there are "higher lives" of countless deities: Buddhas, daos, and gods who differ only in their cultivation methods and appearances. Although they are "incorporeal" (*wuxing*), the deities can assume human form if they so choose, except that their skin is poreless, smooth, and fine. They know everything, including the thoughts of all living beings. They "can become very big"—a buddha's leg is larger than earth itself—and display "powerful supernatural capabilities." One such ability is the elimination of all the diseases of humankind by a simple wave of a buddha's hand. The deities are also responsible for the ozone hole over Antarctica. In actuality, the hole is a "window" opened by the gods to ventilate earth's polluted and poisoned air. More important, the deities "control" (*caozong*) the world and the development of mankind because, as Li put it, "nothing happens by chance, the gods watch over all."[10]

The deities are charged with different functions, such as overseeing reincarnation, the progression of societies, the rotation of the earth, and the very air we breathe. The gods in the microscopic worlds within grains of sand are not confined there but can cross over to the larger world of human beings. "After all," Li explained, "he is a Buddha, he can become as large as the Milky Way Galaxy. When he becomes small, he simply vanishes from sight." Although they wield immense power over human beings, the deities have little regard for humans and generally have nothing to do with them. Human beings, to the gods, are mere "microorganisms" akin to "worms that crawl and live in the dirt."[11]

Among the many and various deities, the lowest level of buddhas are closest to humankind because they had once been "ordinary people." Although the buddhas were not created to save humanity, their compassion has prompted them to bequeath to humans a way to achieve deliverance. Chief among the buddhas is Sakyamuni, the founder of Buddhism, who, it is claimed, was directly reincarnated from his "heavenly kingdom in the sixth layer of universe" to become a man named Gautama Siddhartha, with the express purpose of teaching the Dharma and saving people. So dedicated is Sakyamuni to his salvific mission that he eschewed ascension to paradise (the "original home"), dwelling instead in a place called "Dafan Heaven" within the "Three Realms." From there, he watches over and guides his disciples, whom he has marked with the fylfot or swastika symbol.[12]

There are other buddhas besides Sakyamuni. They include the

seven "primitive buddhas" who preceded Sakyamuni, as well as Buddha Amitabha, Bodhisattva Guanyin, and Bodhisattva Dashizhi. The latter three are "buddhas with human forms" who either constitute or dwell on a huge mountain at the edge of the outermost layer of the cosmos. Called Sumeru Mountain, it is "the manifestation of the form and image" of those three deities. Inside the mountain is "the World of Ultimate Bliss"—heaven by any other name. Aside from buddhas, daos, and gods, angelic beings also seem to be part of the celestial pantheon. In one of his lectures, Li spoke of a disciple who had seen with his "celestial eye" (*tianmu*) "beauties from heaven . . . scattering flowers around, etc."[13]

Matter and Life

In this very complex cosmos, the most elemental matter, according to Li, is composed of "molecules and even more microscopic particles." The latter, at least those known to modern science, include atoms, neutrons, atomic nuclei, electrons, quarks, and neutrinos. "What is further down is unknown to current science," which in any event "cannot be considered as science" because it had been developed "on a wrong basis with flawed understanding."[14] Unknown to science, the actual "origin" (*benyuan*) of matter and thus, of the universe, is water. As Li explained:

> Whenever the most microscopic substance of different levels has reached a certain extent, there is no more matter. . . . If one looks further, one discovers . . . something quiet and still, where no material particles can be seen, something I usually call dead water, which is also called the origin or lifeless water. When you throw something into it, no ripples appear. Sound vibrations do not cause waves. It is completely still. . . . When you squeeze and squeeze leafy

vegetables . . . until nothing is left, all that remains is
water. . . . Even steel and iron can be squeezed into
water . . . bones and hair are composed of water molecules. . . . Actually they are all water. . . . It is water that
forms everything, that has made everything.[15]

As for the origin of life, although Li acknowledged the question
to be extremely complicated, he nevertheless proffered an account.
According to him, the "primordial cosmos" was much simpler and
homogeneous, without so many vertical or horizontal planes as
today. In the course of the motion and evolution of the primordial
cosmos, "life was generated." Then as now, the universe is alive.
Everything—not just humans, animals, and plants—is alive. Even
seemingly inanimate objects are alive. More than simply being alive,
they are also conscious. As Li maintains, "All matter in the universe . . . are living things with minds." Among them are trees,
which "have very advanced thinking activities." This animistic universe, however, can be seen only when one's third or celestial eye is
opened. Only then will one "find that everything including rocks
and walls can talk and greet you."[16]

Humankind and the Fall

In this mega-cosmos, unimaginable in its immensity, "the Earth is
nothing but a speck of dust, just negligible." Despite that, the most
important forms of life on earth are human beings because nothing
would exist without them. As Li wrote, "Precisely because of the
existence of human beings, everything else exists on this Earth." All
animals, creatures, and plants are to be used by man because "everything on Earth is created for human beings."[17]

The special status accorded human beings may be due to their
having been created by the gods. Despite being rather demure on
that subject, saying, "we won't talk about how man is created specif-

ically," Li intimated that the gods created humankind. According to Li: "for a God at the very high level, a mere thought can create you. . . . Buddhas can create your internal organs . . . instantly with just a thought. Once an object is formed, a life is infused." Being the creations of gods, it is not surprising that human beings did not originate on earth. Unlike other living things that "are created here . . . on the earth," human beings alone trace their origins to "the highest levels of the universe."[18]

Exactly what those "high levels" are is not clear, although Li was unambiguous as to why humans no longer live there—it was their moral depravity that led to their fall from the heights. In the "paradise" of the primordial cosmos, he recounted, "no bad things existed at that time." Instead, the earliest human life was fundamentally good, being "assimilated with the characteristic of the universe upon birth." But as increasing numbers of human beings "emerged," some began to "deviate more and more from the cosmic qualities" by becoming selfish and "bad." No longer meeting the standards of the high levels, humans fell to a lower level. Persisting in their immorality, they fell to still lower levels until they reached earth—"to this level of ordinary people in the end." Li further wrote: "At this level, such a person should have been destroyed and eliminated. Yet, out of their great benevolent compassion, those great enlightened people specially created such a space just like this one of our human society. In this dimension of space, he is given this extra human flesh body as well as this extra pair of eyes that can only see matter in this physical dimension. Namely, he is lost in a maze, and he is not allowed to see the truth of the universe."[19]

Previous Civilizations and UFOs

By asserting that humans did not originate on earth, Li evidently did not subscribe to the Darwinian theory that homo sapiens had evolved from the primates. Citing the hitherto unsuccessful efforts of anthropologists to uncover fossil evidence of the missing links between species, Li stated outright, "we don't believe that evolution occurred." Instead of having evolved from the apes, human beings are what they are because of their fall from goodness, "because you have become bad."[20]

More than that, human beings have existed on earth for far, far longer than is claimed by science, memories of which, Li insisted, are stored in our consciousness. Our present civilization is only the most recent of many human civilizations, each of which was destroyed when society became degenerate and decadent. In Li's words, "Mankind has . . . been constantly . . . re-discovering itself. . . . The planet we inhabit has already experienced destruction many times. . . . [Each time] only a few people survived and lived a primitive life. Then, they would gradually multiply in number to become the new human race and begin a new civilization. Afterwards, they were again exterminated and would once again multiply to be a new human race."[21]

As evidence of those prior human civilizations, Li pointed to the following: the ancient Egyptian pyramids; the Mayans (who were "directly related to the Mongolians"); Noah's ark and the biblical great flood; prehistoric relics in China, which include *I Ching* (*The Book of Changes*), Tai Chi, Bagua (the eight trigrams), and qigong; tall large ancient architecture allegedly discovered under ocean waters; cave frescoes in France, South Africa, and the Alps, some dating back 250,000 years, which depicted people holding smoking pipes and walking sticks, dressed in Western suits, hats, and tight pants; a two-billion-year-old uranium ore in the Gabon Republic of Africa; an ancient iron rod in India with a 99-percent iron purity that exceeds the capabilities of modern smelting technology; a 30,000-year-old rock in the National University of Peru Museum, engraved with a human figure observing the heavens through a telescope; and a fossilized rock in which a human shoe print and a trilobite are found together, despite the fact that trilobites had been extinct for 260 million years. None of this, Li insisted, can be explained by Darwin's theory of evolution because "how could human beings have possibly produced such things at a time when they themselves might have been micro-organisms?"[22]

Without explicitly calling it Atlantis, Li maintained that one of those earlier civilizations "on the periphery" of continental Europe was destroyed when it "sank under water during a continental change." Later, new continents were created, emerging from the oceans. The last human civilization had been destroyed by a great flood, making the story of Noah's ark true. During that flood, Western culture was completely destroyed, which would explain why Caucasians today have "no civilization at all" because they had "developed from nothing." In contrast, rural people and the "mountain people" who lived in the Himalayan and Kunlun Mountains "luckily survived." Chinese were among those mountain people of Kunlun, which would account for China's prehistoric cultural relics of I Ching, Tai Chi, Bagua, Hetu, Luoshu, qigong, and "ancient Chinese science" in general which, Li insisted, was and remains far superior to modern Western science.[23]

Echoing the writings of the 1940s science fiction writer Richard S. Shaver, Li maintained that those humans who were "selected out" (*taotai*) in past apocalypses went underground to live below the earth's surface.[24] Others went into the oceans, where they developed fishlike upper torsos while retaining humanoid lower bodies. Although they have human "sentiments" (*qing*), they are devoid of "desires and passions" (*yu*).[25]

According to Li, some of earth's ancient civilizations had been highly advanced. Among their accomplishments was the creation of the moon to provide light in the evening sky. After each apocalypse, the few survivors salvaged a portion of the prehistoric culture and began a new stone age. Drawing from the results of his "careful investigation" into this matter, Li concluded that humanity had undergone "complete annihilation" eighty-one times. More than that, our universe itself is "a reconstructed entity" after having experienced nine "catastrophic explosions." As Li explained: "Each time when earth reached its final stage, life had become impure and debased. . . . Earth itself was a big ball of karma and was obliterated. . . . But there were still some good people, though very few in number . . . who survived and were moved to another planet. . . . The gods then re-created human beings (*ren*), albeit with different appearances."[26]

The survivors of earth's destruction who were transported to another planet brought with them their extant technology so that they were able to begin anew at "a comparatively high starting point." In addition to these transplants, there are also other intelligent beings in the universe who are indigenous to their planets. In fact, Li maintained, "There is life on every star and planet. It is just that we can't see them because they are not in our dimension." Over the course of eons, the transplanted "space people" (*waixing ren*) continued to develop, and their accumulated knowledge of the universe far surpassed that of ours today. Their bodies can enter into other dimensions, and their spaceships can navigate in other space-time continua at a speed unimaginable to us, using fuel that is beyond our comprehension or capabilities. Despite their technological advancements, they remain morally underdeveloped. Their greed and "lust" (*yuwang*) fomented conflict, which led to "star wars." Happily, earth has not been targeted in those wars because the space people are not threatened by us. All that will change, however, if and when human beings become sufficiently powerful to pose a threat.[27]

In the meantime, the space people had been systematically preparing to occupy earth and take over humanity. Covetous of our "most perfect" bodies, they initiated their full-scale invasion of earth at the time of the "white man's" industrial revolution. According to Li: "Human beings believe that they are the sole life in the universe, which is so pathetic, so very pathetic. Aliens have visited our earth and there are even photos as proof, yet people still do not believe in their existence. . . . Flying saucers from other planets can travel directly in other dimensions . . . come and go at will and at a speed that is so fast that the human minds cannot accept it."[28]

In an interview in 1999 with *Time* magazine, Li expounded further on the space aliens who have visited earth. Sounding like an episode of *The X-Files,* Li maintained that extraterrestrials first came to earth circa 1900. "One type of alien looks like a human but has a nose made of a bone," he confided, while others resembled ghosts. The aliens provided humankind with science and its many inventions, such as computers and airplanes. But they have a nefarious agenda: they taught us science in order to render us abjectly dependent on technology. Everything we learn, from grade school to college, is their science, as is everything we use. As Li put it, "How else can one explain the rapid advancements in our computer and other technologies?" Seduced by their science and technology, human beings have become automatons, each of us reduced to being just a number. Some of the space people have married earthlings (without the earthlings' knowledge of their identities, of course); others are in hiding. Still others are inside our bodies, a prospect that Li exclaimed to be "most frightening!" The space people's ultimate objective is to completely assimilate us, exchange our "souls" (*yuanshen*), and "replace all humans with clones."[29]

Toward that purpose, the space people had selected a few nations to be their "forerunner and vanguard" (*xiandao*). They are: Japan, their vanguard in technology; the United States, in culture (via the destruction of the ancient cultures of the world and replacing them with American pop culture); England, in machine production; and Spain, in "race mixing" (*hunza renzhong*). According to

Li, Spain has already produced the mongrel races of contemporary South Americans, Central Americans, Mexicans, and Southeast Asians. By their racial crossbreeding, human beings are abandoning the gods and becoming rootless. More than that, Li warned, a person of mixed blood has lost her corresponding bodies in the other dimensions. As Li said, "for yellow people, there are yellow people above, for white people, there are white people above." A person of mixed races, however, "has lost this thread."[30]

Li acknowledged that what the space people have done and intend to do to humans is clearly immoral. Although more powerful than human beings, the space people are still subject to the moral dicta of the universe. Given that, Li inquired, what can account for their temerity in dealing with humans? His answer is that although "none of this escapes the eyes of the gods," sadly, "the gods no longer care" (*shen buguanle*).[31]

Moral Law

Li's assertion that human beings had fallen to earth because they were bad can only mean that the universe is governed by certain moral principles. As he observed, the universe "does not only have its material existence," it is fundamentally moral in character. Simply put, there is "*Fa* (law) in this universe" because the universe "is constrained by reason (*li*)".[32]

That law is comprised of *zhen, shan,* and *ren* (truth, benevolence, and forbearance), which are at once the nature, composition, and characteristic of the universe, as well as the source of all other moral virtues. All matter in the universe assumes forms of this law at different levels, to which human beings are subject because our ordinary human society must progress according to the law of history. As Li put it, "society develops independent of one's will. Nobody can determine its course." Li further explained: "Life is benevolent. . . . There is the characteristic of Zhen (truth, truth-fulness)-Shan (benevolence, kindness, compassion)-Ren (endur-ance, forbearance, tolerance) in the tiny particles of air, rock, wood, soil, iron and steel, the human body, as well as in all matter. . . . *This characteristic of Zhen-Shan-Ren is the sole criterion for determining what is good or bad.* . . . As a human being, if you follow . . . Zhen-Shan-Ren, you are a good person. One who goes against this char-acteristic is genuinely a bad person."[33]

More than being a moral law that enables us to "distinguish good from evil, and right from wrong," *Fa* is also "the most myste-rious, profound, and superior science (*kexueh*) of all the theories in the world." For it is only through *Fa* that "myths of the universe, time-space, and the human body are completely unveiled." How-ever advanced human society becomes in scientific and technologi-cal prowess, if we do not understand *Fa,* the truth of the universe will forever remain elusive. As Li puts it, "the Buddha Fa covers everything . . . from a grain or particle to the universe, from the smallest to the biggest." It "sees through all mysteries, includes everything, leaving out nothing." Only it "can fully explain human-ity, matter . . . and the whole universe."[34]

It is here (and in other places) that Li Hongzhi revealed the syncretic nature of his belief system. In the first place, the symbols that he chose for his sect are Buddhist (the swastika or fylfot) and Daoist (the swirling Tai Chi icon). His writings and lectures are liberally sprinkled with references to Siddhartha, the founder of Buddhism, and Laozi, the progenitor of Daoism. More important, Li identified the universal law he teaches as "what Daoists call the Way, what Buddhists call Fa." He even explicitly identified Falun Gong as "a Buddhist sect" (*fomen*).[35]

At the same time, however, he insisted that his teachings actu-ally are more complete than, and thus superior to, either Buddhism or Daoism. As he put it, "this thing that we are cultivating is very big and exceeds the boundaries of Buddhism itself." He contended that traditional Buddhism managed to plumb only a very small portion of the Great Law. Most significantly, neither Daoism nor Buddhism addresses all three of the universe's moral principles. Whereas Daoism emphasizes *zhen* (truthfulness) and Buddhism preaches *shan* (benevolence or compassion), only Li's Falun Dafa teaches all three of the universe's moral principles by including *ren* (tolerance or forbearance). As Li said, "The Fa we are teaching today exceeds the conventional understanding of the Buddha Fa. . . . The *dafa* that I teach today is . . . the law of the universe."[36]

Karma

If the universe is governed by moral laws, so too are human beings. Li wrote: "When gods created human beings, they were provided with rules (*guifan*) governing their behavior and lifestyle. Those who exceed these [moral] boundaries cannot be called human." As human beings, we have the freedom of will to be good or bad. This free will was described by Li as: "If you say, 'I want to become a Buddha through cultivation', then the Buddha might help you. . . . On the other hand, if one wants to be a demon, no one can stop him either. . . . Thus, one's wish is of paramount importance."[37]

Whether we choose goodness or evil, our actions have consequences. This is because the universe operates on an absolute unchanging principle—a sort of moral analog of the physics law of interaction, whereby for every action, there is an equal and opposite reaction. As articulated by Li, this principle is one of "to gain, you must lose; if you owe [a debt], you must repay."[38]

In human beings, the universal principle expresses itself as virtue and karma: those who have done good attain *de* (virtue); those who have committed evil accumulate *yeli* (karma). (In fact, Li states that another name for karma is what Jesus called sin.) According to Li, "There is a field that surrounds a human body. . . . This field is the De . . . a white substance [that] . . . is attained when we have suffered pains, endured setbacks, and have done good deeds while the black substance [karma] is collected when one commits sins and wrong deeds."[39]

An individual with a lot of *de* will attain whatever he wants and enjoy great success in life. One who has incurred karma, however, will experience "difficulties, suffering, hardships, lack of money, and many illnesses" not just in this life, but also in the next. This is because, as Li explained, "Your body is like the annual rings of a tree, life after life, karma starts from the very center and exists in every layer. . . . Good things are passed along, and so are bad things." For that matter, it is impossible not to have karma because simply "to live is to incur karma." As an example, every time we open our mouths to speak, our words may inadvertently hurt others. In order to live, we must eat, which necessarily involves killing of animals or plants. Just the simple act of walking entails killing because we cannot help but step on vegetation, insects, and microscopic organisms invisible to our eyes.[40]

Karma and virtue are not only carried over from past lives, they are also inherited. As Li said, "they can be built up from ancestors" because when an individual dies after incurring karma, his "descendants must repay this karma." Happily, virtue is also inherited in that a virtuous person can "bequeath" good fortune to her offspring and progeny. This passing of karma also works in reverse direction: just as the sins of the father are visited upon the son, the son's virtue can spillover to benefit his parents.[41]

In effect, in Li's conception of the universe, misfortunes are not something that just happen. Instead, we create our own misfortune through the evil we have done. Sickness, therefore, is both an indicator as well as the result of bad deeds committed in this or some previous life. As Li put it, "present-day science cannot see the fundamental causes of what makes people ill. . . . There are people who are destined to suffer from disease. . . . The fundamental cause for the illness . . . is the karma accumulated life after life."[42]

Indeed, Li's conception of the etiology of disease is quite complicated. According to him, the "white substance" of *de* is "assimilated" with the universe's moral virtues (those of *zhen-shan-ren*). An individual with a lot of *de* will enjoy good health because "the characteristic of the universe can be directly manifested in your body and will communicate with your body." In contrast, one who has karma will be alienated from the beneficent forces of the universe. "When this black substance is accumulated to a great amount, it will form a field surrounding one's body, which will wrap him inside," resulting in sickness. A small amount of karma will be "reflected" as "disease poison" (*bingdu*); a great deal of karma, however, will manifest itself as "germs or bacteria" (*xijun*).[43]

The nature and etiology of disease prompted Li to counsel his followers who have achieved the supernormal ability to cure sicknesses to refrain from so doing. In attempting to cure someone's illness, Li warned, not only might the healer take on the patient's "black" energy (*qi*), the healer is also denying the patient the opportunity, via suffering, to clear her karma. The result is that although the patient may appear to be cured, she will still have to repay her karma by enduring other forms of hardship and suffering. As Li observed, "It is because of the karma resulted from committing wrong deeds in the past that one will have illnesses or tribulations, and suffering is repaying the debt of karma. Thus, nobody can change it. Changing it will mean that one does not have to repay the debt. . . . When you are suffering from an illness, your karma is truly being removed. You will recover once such removal is over. . . . People . . . think it is bad to suffer even a little bit. Actually, what is so terrible about suffering? To be a human being is to suffer."[44]

Not only should Li's disciples eschew healing the sick, they should also refrain from interfering in others' affairs in general because the truth is not readily evident. For example, when we see one person punching another with his fist, what appears to be an act of aggression may actually be "an act of clearing a karmic debt." By interfering, we "are probably hindering them in the settlement of their karmic debt." Instead, such matters should be left to "worldly law" to adjudicate between right and wrong and "take care of matters of gratitude and resentment."[45]

Reincarnation, Soul, Predestination, and Parallel Lives

The concept of karma implies reincarnation. It is Li's contention that people can be reincarnated not just as human beings, but also as animals in the next lifetime. An animal, however, will have to wait "several hundreds or thousands of years" to be reincarnated as a human being. We may even be reincarnated as a piece of rock, which would make repaying one's karma nearly impossible because "if that piece of rock is not smashed or weathered away, you will never be able to come out."[46]

The concept of reincarnation, in turn, implies the existence of a soul, something that persists after the death of the physical body. In his writings and seminars, Li made reference to human beings' "original" or "chief spirit" (*yuanshen*) that seems to possess all the attributes of a soul. In a seminar in New York on March 22, 1997, responding to a question from a disciple, Li Hongzhi asserted that an individual's chief spirit usually enters the body not long before birth. The time of entry, however, is not fixed. As he put it, "Maybe it's the moment before birth, maybe it's long before birth, half a month, a month, or even earlier, all are possible." Whereas the biological parents have begotten their child's "body of flesh," they did not create the child's soul or "life" (*shengming*).[47] The latter is a matter for the gods.

Some of Li's followers reported having out-of-body experiences when their chief spirits "floated" out of their bodies. For ordinary people, however, the soul leaves the body only when he or she dies. When that happens, Li recounted, the chief spirit will come out of the body "like a breeze of smoke drifting about" and will be reincarnated into another body, bringing with it the karma and virtues accumulated in its previous life. In effect, what human beings call "death" is merely the demise of the physical body because our original spirit "does not become extinct," except in the case of someone who has committed "all kinds of evil deeds" and incurred so much karma that both his body and soul became "extinct" and all his cells "disintegrate."[48]

It is because human beings have an immortal soul that Li disapproves of abortion. That, to him, is killing—an act that, like other forms of killing, would incur a "quite large" karmic debt. He also opposes human cloning because "even if a clone were made, it wouldn't be that person. Only demons can get into him and God won't give him a spirit."[49]

And it is not just human beings who have souls: everything, animate and seemingly inanimate, has a soul. According to Li, "when any object is created, a life enters it . . . [even a] product made by a factory." The only difference between humans and other animals is that only human beings, "being the greatest," can become "God or Buddha through cultivation"—an avenue that is not available to other creatures because they lack the human spirit. Animals are thus prohibited by nature from "cultivating." An animal that defies this law of nature and cultivates must be killed before it turns into a "demon" (*mo*).[50]

Li also maintains that our lives, as well as our relationships, are predestined (*yuan* or *yuanfen*). According to him, "when a person is born, a complete profile of his lifetime will exist"—where his life is and what he should do—all of which having been prearranged by "a higher life." Although an individual can try to change his (pre-destined) life, he cannot change "big events."[51]

The concept of predestination also includes predestined relationships. Li maintained that an individual's *yuan* involves a very long period of time, more than one or even several lifetimes. Just as karma and virtue are passed from one life to the next, "the causal relationships among people do not end either." There are individuals with whom one has no *yuanfen:* "such people . . . seem to be on a different path from yours." Then there are those "from your group," for whom one is predestined: "Some will be parents, some will be children, some will be friends, some will be enemies, and some will be benefactors." Li believes that those individuals who are attracted to his teachings and became his disciples had been predestined to do so. As Li informs his followers, "Everyone comes here because of predestined relationship."[52]

More than human affairs, the universe itself is predestined in that in "its formative beginnings, it already carried within itself the plan (*anpai*) for its end." Li maintains that it was not an accident that qigong, including Falun Gong, became so popular in China in recent years because such phenomena are characteristic of the impending arrival of the "end times" (*mojie*).[53]

More than reincarnation, human beings also have parallel lives. These are one's other selves who live in the other dimensions of the universe. As Li describes it:

> As human beings we have a body in each of numerous dimensions. . . . The body in another dimension can become large or small. . . . When a person is born, there are many of him born simultaneously within a certain territory of this cosmic space. They all look alike with the same name, and they do similar things. . . . If one of them is suddenly dead while the rest of him in various other

dimensions have not yet completed their predestined journey of life with still many years to live, this dead person
will . . . wander around . . . until everyone of him in each
dimension completes his journey of life.[54]

Law Wheel Cultivation

As human beings, we are "in a maze" because of the Fall and must
practice cultivation so that we may "return to our original true
selves" (*fanben guizhen*). Li calls this "returning to the truth,"
to "the primordial state" before the Fall, to our "place of origin"—
the "higher level" where there is no suffering. As he puts it, "a person's life is not meant to be just a human being." Only by recover-
ing our true selves can "the human problem" be "fundamentally
resolved."[55]

The cultivation that is needed is that of falun gong. Li was
candid in stating that the purpose of his sect is to save people by
helping them to return to their true selves. Salvation requires that
one repay the debt of karma that is "owed to the gods" because the
universe's "principle" demands that bad deeds be repaid. Even
Jesus could not redeem humanity from its collective karma. He had
tried to die for our sins by taking our karma upon himself, but the
accumulated karma was so immense that in the end, he could not
even "free" (*jietou*) himself. Only by dying on the cross—by abandoning his body—was he freed.[56]

Accordingly, human salvation can only take place on an individual basis by each person undertaking Falun Gong's cultivation practice. Only through cultivation practice, Li insists, "can . . . [one's]
life be changed" and the individual attain "genuine freedom." By
practicing Falun Dafa, one's karma will be "abolished" and with it,
illnesses will be cured and good health ensured.[57] More than that,
the practice of falun gong will eventually result in the practitioner's

attainment of enlightenment, at which time she will be transformed into nothing less than a living god.

Cultivation Practice

By "cultivation practice" (*xiulian*) Li seems to refer to three separate but interrelated enterprises. The first is the "practice" (*lian*) of falun gong—a simpler but nevertheless allegedly superior version of traditional qigong devised by Li. As he describes it, "Falun Gong is a special cultivation way of the Buddha School . . . different . . . [and] much superior to other cultivation ways in terms of what it offers."[58]

Five sets of exercises comprise Li's brand of qigong. The first set is called "Buddha Showing the Thousand Hands." These are basic exercises designed to "stretch body and mind." The second set is called "Falun Standing Stance," a series of exercises that uses slow, tranquil movements lasting for minutes at a time. The third set is "Penetrating the Two Cosmic Extremes," exercises that allegedly meld one's body with the cosmos. The fourth set is "Falun Heavenly Circulation," which Li claims is the best way to circulate energy between the yin and yang sides of the body. A fifth and last set is called "Strengthening Supernormal Powers." These are "paranormal-enhancing" exercises that had been secrets but, happily, are now "declassified."[59]

Performing these exercises, Li claims, will improve one's *xinxing* (literally, heart nature), which he defines as "mind-nature" and "moral quality." How that process works is that the "black substance" or karma within an individual is turned into the "white substance" of virtue (*de*) that, in turn, is transformed into "cultivation energy" (*gong*). As the practitioner cultivates, her *gong* will form an "energy column" (*gongzhu*) above her head, which will grow higher and higher as she ascends to higher planes of cultivation.[60]

Exercises alone, however, will not be sufficient. There is also a cognitive dimension to cultivation: the practitioner must also study Falun Dafa to learn the truth of the universe. According to Li, "once such a person studies our Falun Dafa, he will suddenly understand many questions which he wished to understand, but could not find an answer to in the past [and] . . . he will become very excited."[61]

At the same time, in addition to the exercises and the learning of the Great Law, there is also a moral dimension to Falun Gong. As Li himself admits, his teachings are aimed at making people "good" by assimilating them into the universe's moral qualities of *zhen-shan-ren*. Once the practitioner is assimilated, she will have attained the Way (*Dao*), "it is as simple as that."[62]

Moral cultivation requires the practitioner to directly upgrade her moral standard by "cultivating" (*xiu*) her soul (*yuanshen*) and "tempering" her heart. As Li instructs, "If you want to reach a higher level, you must give up your ill thoughts and clean up your filthy stuff to assimilate with the requirement standard of that level." In this way, by striving to be good, the practitioner will continuously upgrade her moral level.[63]

Li understands a virtuous person to be an individual who "has very good inborn qualities," "great forbearance," "very good enlightenment quality," and who "takes the worldly things very lightly." The latter refers to the surrendering ("putting down") of all the "attachments" (*zhizhu*) that make us human. Attachments refer to our desires for things that we "cannot give up," including sex, meat-eating, alcohol, cigarettes, material goods, money, human relationships, *qing* (sentiments, affections, desires, and passions—including filial piety), and life and death. As Li expresses it, "Having obtained the Fa, I fear no life and death and can even give up my life."[64]

Transformation

In the course of the cultivation practice, the practitioner's physical body "will go through tremendous changes," and according to Li, she "will give up those bad things"that she was attached to. After her body has become purified, as Li puts it, she will begin to "attract small animals."[65]

As the practitioner ascends to higher planes, she becomes increasingly "assimilated to the cosmos" and will develop "supernormal abilities," which Li sees as the "instinctual abilities of the human body" that had degenerated as human society became more and more developed. The practitioner's third or "celestial" eye will open. That eye, according to Li, is "located slightly above and between one's eyebrows" and is connected to the pineal gland. The eye's initial opening is described by Li as follows: "People usually practice . . . at midnight when the night is dark and quiet. As one practices, he will suddenly see a large eye before his eyes. . . . That large unblinking eye is looking, and it is vividly clear. Accordingly, some people call it the demon's eye . . . others call it the Buddha's eye, etc. In fact, it is your own eye."[66]

The celestial eye enables the practitioner to see what X-ray, CT, and "supersonic" scanners see—and more. With it, a practitioner can see through human bodies and walls as well as many otherwise invisible phenomena, including "other time-spaces" and Li Hongzhi's "Law bodies" (*fashen*—apparently images of Li) that are standing "just beside" the practitioner. A practitioner will also be able to see Li's books as "very colorful and golden shiny," with each word in the book bearing the image of his law bodies. One of his disciples claimed to have seen, with his third eye, a golden halo three feet high above Li's head and "a lot of other halos" behind him.[67]

The practitioner will also become clairvoyant, seeing, with the help of a rotating mirror in her forehead, "what someone else is doing in another city." And when the practitioner has ascended to the level of "Wisdom Eyesight," a "breakthrough" will occur. She will look at objects and find "they have all disappeared." As Li describes it, "Nothing exists. Namely, in this particular dimension you will find that people no longer exist."[68]

Other supernormal powers include those of not getting wet in the rain, the "celestial ear," psychokinesis, teleportation, "psychic travel," "transmigration," "fixing power," levitation, and *suming tong*. Transmigration is the ability of a practitioner to "suddenly disappear, and then all of a sudden emerge somewhere else." This is because the highly cultivated body, being "composed of extremely fine grains," "can go through spaces." A practitioner with "fixing power" has the ability, upon seeing "an evildoer running away," to "just say 'fix' and he will be fixed on the spot." Levitation ("flying in the air") is a supernormal ability that is developed "once the great heavenly circuit is opened up." Practitioners, however, must refrain from levitating in public because doing so would disturb the state of ordinary human society. As for *suming tong*, that is the ability to tell the past and future of another person. Those practitioners with a great capability can even predict the rise and fall of society as well as changes in the laws of the cosmos.[69]

Altogether, according to Li, there are "over ten thousand genuine supernormal capabilities." Alas, practitioners must not use these abilities to change human society although Li does permit his disciples to use them in private. This is because "genuine great powers are not allowed to be performed in public, due to their serious consequences and dangers" when they "disturb the normal state of human society." Nor are the supernormal capabilities scientifically verifiable because our "space-time" is different from the space-time where those capabilities exist. "As a result," Li avers, "if scientists who study the human body deduct and conduct research based upon conventional theories as well as modern science, they will waste their efforts even after another ten thousand years because these are something beyond ordinary people anyway."[70]

The "great heavenly circuit" that, when opened, enables the practitioner to levitate is merely "the beginning step" in cultivation practice; more wonders follow. If one continues cultivating, "all the pulses" in a practitioner's body will open up until they are "connected all together . . . to become one piece." The body will no longer have any pulse or acupuncture point and will have been "completely transformed by the high-energy matter." By this time, the practitioner has reached the highest level of cultivation when the human "flesh body" reaches its ultimate limit. The practitioner will be brought into another state in which all the potential human supernormal capabilities emerge. As Li describes it, "a large eye will appear in the upper section of the face, and it has numerous small eyes in it." In addition, some people will also have "eyes all over their bodies, and their sweat pores will have all become eyes." Those eyes will allow the practitioners to read with their ears and see with their hands, feet, stomach, and "from the back of their heads." Others will "carry images of Bodhisattva or Buddha all over their bodies" as well as "many living beings that will become visible."[71]

By this time, the practitioner will have reached the state of "Three Flowers Above the Head" (*sanhua juding*). Rotating clockwise or counterclockwise above the practitioner's head are three "extraordinarily beautiful" flowers that include a lotus and two other flowers, all of which are not of "our physical dimension." Each flower is supported by a huge pole as thick as the diameter of the flower, reaching "all the way to the top of heaven." "You will be scared," Li warns, "if you can see them." Fortunately, the flowers and the poles can be seen only by the third eye.[72]

By this time, the practitioner has reached the highest form of cultivation. Her skin will have become "delicate" and her body "white and pure." The elderly will have their physical strength restored and have very few wrinkles, and women will again menstruate (although, happily, the menstrual flow "will not be much"). Both the aged and the young "will all feel that their entire bodies are light." Moreover, all "will look young and will stay that way in the end."[73]

According to Li, many of his disciples have reached the Three

Flowers stage, but none has yet reached the final stage of "completion or consummation" (*yuanman*). To do that, the practitioner must continue to move forward to arrive at "the ultimate end" when her body will reach "the absolute purity of the highest degree." Made completely of *gong* ("high-energy matter"), the practitioner's body (when seen with the third eye) will be transparent "just like . . . glass, and there is nothing in it." At this point, according to Li, her body "has already become a Buddha's body." Paradoxically, "all supernormal capabilities and supernatural powers will be abandoned all at once . . . put into a very deep dimension as they will become useless and will be no longer of any use from now on." The practitioner will then begin cultivation practice "all over again" and again develop supernormal capabilities.[74]

In effect, the final goal of cultivation practice is to "become God or Buddha." Having surrendered all our attachments, the mind becomes empty. Not only are our bodies in this dimension (which Li calls *zhu yuanshen:* chief spirits) transformed into a Buddha's body, the bodies in all the other dimensions (which he calls *fu yuanshen:* secondary spirits) also "are all changing." As Li says, "When a cultivator has attained the Way . . . and achieved enlightenment, he will belong to the category of the enlightened or supernatural beings." For what is god but a being that is free of human attachments? To maintain that status, however, the cultivator must continue "to do good things all the time." If he commits evil, "he will come down again" and cease to be a god. Worse still, his "life will be in danger immediately."[75]

Life as a god who still lives in human society, however, will not be easy. Although the advanced cultivator will be blessed with good health and a long extended life, it is a lonely life. As described by Li:

You'll find that those who have a common language with you are very few. On this score alone, you'll feel very lonely and find it kind of bitter in your heart. . . . You seem to have less common words and less contacts with ordinary people, even including your family members. . . . But this is all normal . . . because . . . you are more of a God than an ordinary person . . . [and] are not attached to what human beings are attached to; you'll get bored by what human beings take delight in talking about. . . . You'll know everything that others are thinking. Then, you cannot put up with a single thought of others . . . and you feel annoyed.[76]

Li as Divine

If Li Hongzhi's disciples can become gods by engaging in falun gong, it stands to reason that the founder of this cultivation practice must himself be a deity. This conclusion can be reached not just by inference; it is supported by Li's own words. A practitioner's cultivation requires more than the performance of exercises, the learning of the Great Law, and moral improvement. It also depends on the rotation of the "law wheel" (*falun*) that is implanted by Master Li himself into the practitioner's body. The wheel is "the concrete manifestation" of the universe's Great Law and reportedly takes the shape of a left-handed swastika. As Li explains: "I released Falun and planted it in your lower abdomen. Of course, this is done not in this physical space, but in another space . . . having nothing to do with this world."[77]

Despite the wheel not being in "this physical space," Li maintains that those who are very sensitive can feel it rotating, or they may feel "somewhat uncomfortable, a pain in the abdomen or something moving or burning." Highly advanced practitioners possessed of supernormal capabilities can actually see the wheel in their abdomens. Li provides law wheels of different sizes to different practitioners, according to their levels of cultivation. Once implanted by the master, the wheel "keeps revolving automatically . . . absorbing and evolving the ethereal energy incessantly, which is then transformed into cultivation energy." Even if the practitioner occasionally skips the exercises, she is still cultivating because, as Li assures, "all you need to do is done by Falun."[78]

In addition to the implantation (as well as the turning on) of the law wheel, Li is also responsible for the transformation of the practitioner's cultivation energy, a task only he can effectuate. As he explains: "Cultivation depends upon the individual himself while the transformation of Gong is up to the master. . . . It is the master who actually does such a thing as you cannot do it at all. The whole transformation process of cultivation energy is a very complicated one. . . . The body does not only change in just . . . one dimension, but in all dimensions. . . . Can you do that by yourself? You cannot. Such things are arranged by the master as well as performed by the master."[79]

Li's powers go beyond the transformation of cultivation energy; he can also cure the sick. Before the wheel is placed in the practitioner's abdomen, Li must cleanse her body of the "bad things" while retaining the good ones. Some practitioners after being "adjusted" by Li will find themselves "freed from illness" and reach a state of being "milk-white."[80]

More than that, Li's disciples will be maximally protected while they practice by a "cover" (*chaozi*) that outsiders cannot penetrate. The practitioners will also be safeguarded by Li's "countless" law bodies. As he explains, "although you cannot see me in person, in fact, I am right by your side as long as you practice cultivation . . . protecting you every single moment" until cultivation is completed and the state of buddhahood reached.[81] According to Li, law bodies are formed by his cultivation energy and the Great Law and are found in his photos, books, audiotapes, and videotapes, as well as in Falun Gong's other publications. All of them seem to be extensions and duplicates of Li, albeit with curly blue hair and garbed in saffron. Li's law bodies appear joyful and emit a bright light when a disciple has been good but become severe and stern when she has committed bad deeds.[82] His law bodies are not subject to the physical laws of nature in that they can protect his disciples no matter where they are. As he puts it, "Even if you have gone to Hong Kong, the United States, the moon, or the sun, my Law bodies will still protect you." And although Li had emigrated to the United States, he nevertheless can "release" his powers across thousands of miles to effectuate "remote treatment" of his disciples in China. More than protection, his law bodies can also ensure that his disciple will "find an easy job."[83]

If the above powers do not make Li Hongzhi godlike, his other capabilities surely will. He has claimed that he can fly and walk through walls. In his writings, he has claimed to have the power of exorcism: he can make evil spirits "disappear all at once" by a mere swing of his hand; he can also "clear" a house by removing "bad things" from it and covering the house with "an energy . . . so that no evil things will enter it." Not only does Li install the law wheel in his disciple's abdomen, he also opens the practitioner's celestial eye. As he puts it, "One word of mine will be able to open it." Li is all-knowing, claiming that "my Law bodies know everything you have in mind without being told." He is also all-powerful, able to protect his disciples so that they "will meet with no real danger . . . and no accident is allowed to interfere." More important still, Li can also remove one's karma. As he puts it: "When you are practicing cultivation, I keep on pushing this karma outward from the center; I push, and push, and push, and push until I completely push out the karma for you." For that matter, an individual's karma can be cleansed just by reading one of Li's books.[84]

Finally, Li directly admits his divine nature. He has said he does not need to cultivate because he is without karma. Being without karma, it is no wonder that he is freed from the karmic wheel of incarnations. Responding to a question from a follower who asked, "Who were you in a previous life?" Li replied, "I *was* Li Hongzhi." Li also maintained that human beings do not have law bodies and that only he—as well as buddhas, daos, and gods—have law bodies. Falun Gong practitioners must wait until they have completed their cultivation, and attained buddhahood, to have such bodies.[85]

More than that, not only does Li compare himself to Jesus and Buddha Sakyamuni, he claims to be superior to both because they were enlightened beings who operated only "within a small arena." In contrast, Li operates on a much larger scale, being "not of the universe." It is Li alone who can solve the many problems in the universe's many levels and heavenly bodies, including those of human beings on earth. In order to save humanity, for which he has been preparing "for a very long time," he developed Falun Gong, for which he had no master or teacher. According to Li, "If I cannot save you, nobody else can. . . . There is not anyone who will care about you at all. . . . I am the only one in this entire world who . . . is teaching . . . the Great Law." His offer to humanity to learn the Great Law of the universe—which is "not even known by the gods"—is "earthshaking" in that such an opportunity comes only once "every ten thousand years." Nor will this opportunity be offered indefinitely; in fact, it is already too late. As Li says, "Actually, I no longer propagate (*chuan*) the Great Law, as my time for systematically preaching the law is already passed." But his disciples need not fear, for even when Li is "no longer in this world" (*bu zaishi*), he has not really left because his law bodies remain.[86]

Finally, although Li identifies Falun Gong as being of the Buddha school, he claims to have never read Buddhist scriptures. This undoubtedly is due to the fact that, as he admits, "Boddhisattva Guanyin is actually the manifestation of my Law body" for "I have been a Buddha, Dao, as well as *shen*."[87]

The End Days

In effect, the central mission of Falun Gong is not, as Western media reports portray it, that of healthful exercises; the exercises are only the means to the end of human salvation. Falun Gong's salvific mission is prompted by Li Hongzhi's conviction that we are in the last days.

Just as human civilizations had been destroyed in the past because of immorality, like the followers of the White Lotus and the Eight Trigrams in Chinese history, Li is convinced that the moral decadence of our times is leading to another apocalypse. His writings and speeches are replete with references to the "Dharma-ending period" of "the apocalypse," the "Great Havoc," and the "end times" (*mojie*).[88] Decrying that "human moral standard is declining tremendously" and moral values "deteriorating daily," Li predicted that human civilization will be destroyed because human beings have "mutated" (*bianyi*) and are no longer "up to standard." With the end days approaching, Li has set about disseminating Falun Dafa so as "to provide salvation to mankind . . . in this final period of the Last Havoc."[89]

The causes of moral decay are many. Within China, the post-Mao economic reforms opened the country to interaction with the rest of the world. Although the reforms have introduced many new technologies and improved living standards, "bad things," such as pornography, homosexuality, "sex revolution," drug abuse, and more, have also been imported. As Li describes the conditions in China: "The human society seems to be progressing while it is actually regressing. . . . Especially after joining the high tide of the commodity economy, many people have become morally corrupt and have moved further away from Zhen-Shan-Ren, the characteristic of the universe."[90]

Humankind's moral degradation transcends the boundaries of

China to envelope the world, and the root cause of this is Western knowledge, which has made human beings more and more materialistic. A particular culprit is science and its faulty "understanding of the human race, nature, and matter," all of which has led to "the degeneration of morality in today's human society." In effect, as Li sees the problem, the West is the primary cause of humanity's moral decadence. Western knowledge, together with the decadent Western culture, are the "demons" that "appear in the end times to bring turmoil to . . . society." For humankind to continue along this path would be extremely dangerous because, as Li darkly warns, "When things are at their extreme, there will be the opposite. . . . If mankind does not do something about it, heaven will."[91]

The signs of moral decay in a degenerated human society are everywhere and in all walks of life. They range from the serious to the seemingly trivial and include the following:

- Ethnic problems, "problems between countries," and conflicts within and among nationalities.

- "Social crimes" of drug taking, drug trafficking, drug making, and the underworld.

- Loose sexual mores of homosexuality, transsexuality, sexual liberation, and women's liberation, the latter a reaction by women to being "bullied" by men.

- Social problems that are engendered by women's liberation—those of "divorce, fighting, children being abandoned, etc."

- The perversion of moral values whereby people take "money and fame by force," glorify gangsters and criminals, and mistake "wrong for right, bad for good, evil for benevolence."

- Treating human beings as "worse than dogs" and at the same time "treating dogs as children by feeding them milk," dressing them "in fancy brand-named clothes," and pushing them around in strollers while "many people are begging for food in the street."

- The deterioration of human relations whereby "the philosophy of competition" is advocated and "selfishness and desires have made people wary of each other."

- The triumph of materialism whereby people "dare to do anything for profit and money."

- Advances in science, such as human cloning, which "appear only after the decline of human morality."

- Cultural decay that includes the "so-called modern art," rock and roll, "demonic" disco dance, and the "madness" that seizes sports fans during soccer games.

- "Demonic" youthful fashions that regard all things "dark and gloomy as beautiful," including the way "high school students wear their pants, with belts tied on their buttocks"; hairstyles with "the head . . . shaven clean on both sides, leaving . . . one line of hair in the middle, like devils"; young girls "dressed in black . . . like ghosts in the netherworld"; and "monster-looking toys" that look "ugly and ferocious."[92]

Such signs of decadence, as Li puts it, "emerge in an endless stream" and "penetrate into every aspect of society" because in the absence of moral standards, "human beings may come up with anything." But, Li insists, a human being is more than mere "limbs and trunk"—our humanity is intimately dependent on our morality.

Accordingly, "If a person loses his moral concepts, moral norms, and rules of conduct, he is no longer human." All of which provokes the gods to "no longer treat people as human beings."[93]

In the coming "apocalypse" (*jienan*), good people will be protected. Some people, however, are not "redeemable" and will have to be "destroyed" (*xiaohui*) and "eliminated" (*taotai*) "in a big plague" or an "explosion." The gods will first destroy homosexuals for violating "the rules that were given to humankind." Other "evil people" will also be destroyed "in a horrific manner": Not only will they suffer great pain, their suffering will be prolonged. Human beings, in general, will be "obliterated" because man has "indulged in his demonic nature (*moxing*) by doing whatever he desires," resulting in his having "fallen to the lowest level" instead of "living in openness and light." For that, "he will be thoroughly obliterated from the universe."[94]

Teetering at the edge of the abyss, humankind seems unable to solve its many problems. As Li puts it, "Having no way out, no one can come up with any solutions." Governments are impotent because "no sooner has one phenomenon been kept under control than another appears that is even worse. When they try to control it, an even worse problem arises." To maintain a modicum of order and decency, governments resort to legislation as "an expedient measure when there is nothing further that can be done." But the proliferation of laws succeeds only in restraining human beings "like animals."[95]

Nor are the world's many religions and cults any help because they are also caught in the downward spiral. According to Li, "it is difficult to cultivate within Buddhism now" because Buddhist temples "have become very chaotic . . . in these end times" and even the monks "find it difficult to save themselves." Christianity, though a "proper religion," is equally helpless because "its teachings have been distorted."[96]

In these last days "when all the gods have abandoned them" and neither government nor religion can save humanity, only Li offers a way out. This is because "the root cause for all human ills is the decay of human morality. Without working on this, no human problems can be solved." In this defiled world, the only sanctuary—the "pure region" (*jingtu*)—is Li's Falun Dafa, that "right law" (*zhengfa*) that can constrain people. As he puts it, "The ultimate way out for the human race . . . is to cultivate De (virtue) across the land."[97] But although Li Hongzhi alone can offer deliverance to humanity and is doing his "utmost" to propagate "the right law in these end times," he and his sect are being viciously and openly attacked by "demons." The only consolation is that the good will survive the coming Great Havoc to rebuild the world. As Li assures us, "it is not possible . . . for human society not to exist." Being "the manifestation of the Great Law (Dharma) . . . human society will always exist."[98]

Chapter Four

The State vs. Falun Gong

Admittedly, the beliefs of Falun Gong—concerning earth's previous civilizations, space aliens, multiple dimensions, reincarnation, "three flowers rotating above the head," and so forth—are esoteric and nothing short of extraordinary. One is hard pressed, however, to imagine the belief system, or the group that espouses those beliefs, to be evil. But that is precisely the Chinese government's allegation.

When Beijing banned Falun Gong on July 22, 1999, the prohibition was justified on grounds that the sect was injurious to the well-being of people and society because it had "seriously disturbed the normal order of society, confused the people's moral and ethical concepts, deceived many innocent people and inflicted enormous harm on their physical and mental health." More than that, the sect constitutes nothing less than a systemic threat to China and its government. By jeopardizing the cause of building "socialism with Chinese characteristics," it is claimed, Falun Gong has imperiled social order and stability. In order to protect people and society, the government was convinced it must undertake a serious political struggle against the sect. All of which meant that, in the words of China's official Xinhua News Agency, Falun Gong "must not be allowed to continue to exist and further develop."[1]

In making its case, the Chinese government assembled a daunting array of charges against Falun Gong. The accusations include the following:

- Falun Gong is an evil cult.
- It is harmful to the physical and mental well-being of people.
- It hurts society by disrupting social order and the work of institutions.
- It is superstitious and antiscience.
- It is hypocritical.
- It is criminal.
- It is treasonous.
- It is seditious.
- It is well organized.
- Lastly, in banning and suppressing the sect, the government has acted lawfully and with the best of intentions.

The government's evidence for each of these charges is presented in the following sections.

An Evil Cult

One of the main indictments Beijing made against Falun Gong is that it is an evil cult. As the word is used in the English language, "cult" is considered a mixed word because it is both descriptive and normative: the word does not simply refer to an empirical phenomenon but carries a value connotation that is mainly negative.

Leo Pfeffer, the distinguished jurist and leading American theoretician on religious liberty, once wrote, "if you believe in it, it is religion or perhaps *the* religion; and if you do not care one way or another about it, it is a sect; but if you fear and hate it, it is a cult."[2] Although intended as humor, Pfeffer's characterization contains more than a grain of truth. Whether something is called a religion, sect, or cult seems to depend on one's approbation or disapprobation and, as such, is very much a matter of subjective judgment.

Of the three terms, "cult" is the most problematic. As it is used in the English language, the word has different meanings with varying degrees of normative connotations ranging from positive to the decidedly negative.[3]

A positive definition of cult is that provided by the *Oxford English Dictionary:* "worship; reverential homage rendered to a divine being or beings." This definition comes from the historical theological usage of "cult," which is rarely heard today outside of religious circles.

Definitions that are neutral in their value connotation tend to be sociological, where the emphasis is on the religious group's size and novelty. As examples, "cult" is variously defined as a small religious group that exists in a state of tension with the predominant religion; an innovative, fervent religious group, as contrasted with more established and conventional sects and denominations; any small religious group, no matter what its age or teachings; a small, recently created, religious organization which is often headed by a single charismatic leader and is viewed as a spiritually innovative group; and a new religious movement on its way to becoming a denomination.

Then there are the definitions that are implicitly or explicitly pejorative. As an example, evangelical Christian and countercult movements define "cult" as any religious group that "accepts most but not all of the historical Christian doctrines" and, consequently, is theologically suspect. Similarly, fundamentalist Christians label as "cult" any religious group that deviates from historical Protestant Christian beliefs. For mental health groups and the anti-cult movement, "cult" refers to any group that preaches the imminence of doomsday and exerts mind control over its believers through deceptive practices and the employment of dangerous psychological pressure techniques. Similarly, Western popular media conceives of "cult" as a synonym for a doomsday or a mind-controlling religious group, referring to "a small, evil religious group, often with a single charismatic leader, which engages in brainwashing and other mind control techniques, believes that the end of the world is imminent, and collects large amounts of weaponry in preparation for a massive war."

Given these various meanings of "cult," especially those with negative connotations, civil liberties groups recommend that the word be used rarely and that it be substituted with value-neutral and empirically more precise terms, such as "emergent religion," "new" or "alternative religious movement," or "faith group." An even better recourse, it is proposed, is to simply refer to the group by its name. That same sensibility convinced the Associated Press, in May 1998, to eschew "cult" altogether and replace it with the more neutral term of "sect." One civil liberties group observes that use of the word "cult" without careful definition in advance leads to confusion and misunderstanding. But if one's purpose is "to direct public fear and hatred against a new religious group, then 'cult' is an ideal word to use." Doing so, however, would be both "irresponsible and immoral."[4]

In the case of the Chinese government, by characterizing Falun Gong as an "evil cult," there is little doubt that it is employing the derogatory definition of "cult." As China's national government newspaper, *People's Daily*, put it, "Similar to other evil cults worldwide, Falun Gong idolizes its ringleader, Li Hongzhi, who has carried out spiritual worship for himself and disseminated malicious theories of doomsday and sin eradication among practitioners."[5]

That Beijing's definition of "cult" is a highly negative one is also evident in a volume published by the Chinese Academy of Social Sciences (CASS). In it, a CASS scholar, making the case that Falun Gong is an evil cult, employed a criterial definition of cult as any destructive or extremist worship group that adulates the religious leader who claims to be god and who exploits the group for his own accumulation of wealth; brainwashes believers; propagates the imminence of doomsday; is "anti-society, anti-traditional morality, and anti-human nature"; and has a tight organization.[6]

Another CASS scholar compared Falun Gong to such extremist religious groups as People's Temple and Aum Shinrikyo. According to the writer, Li Hongzhi is just like the leaders of those groups, Jim Jones and Asahara Shoko, respectively. Like them, Li claims to be god and insists that his followers "renounce all other beliefs to worship and obey him in transforming themselves into new men and women." Like those other groups, Falun Gong lies and deceives. It cynically exploits human weaknesses by feigning to be virtuous and caring so as to lure people into joining the cult. In the end, the believers in these groups lost everything—their reason, dignity, and the ability to distinguish right from wrong. They became mentally deranged and despairing of life, society, and government. Many committed suicide or murder or attacked party and government institutions because of the mind control exerted by the sect over its members.[7]

Harmful to People

It is not just CASS scholars who accuse Falun Gong of having caused believers to harm themselves and others, the Chinese government has repeatedly accused the sect of inciting suicides and murders. As an example, when Beijing banned Falun Gong on July 22, 1999, the Chinese Embassy in Washington, D.C., issued a press release asserting that unspecified "facts collected by certain departments" of the government demonstrated that Falun Gong had caused innumerable cases of "dire consequences" to the psychological and physical well-being of people. The harmful effects ranged from the relatively minor problems of paranoia, loss of appetite, and "disorganization" in speech and behavior, to more serious problems of sickness, "handicaps," and family discord, to still more serious problems of deaths from untreated ailments, suicide, and murder.[8]

According to a study allegedly conducted by reporters for Xinhua, erstwhile happy families had been "emotionally destroyed" and "dismembered" by Li Hongzhi's "evil instructions." One of those families was that of Tian Jianguo of Henan province who, along with his wife, began practicing Falun Gong in 1997. Their fifteen-year-old son, Tian Pei, also became a believer and "gradually lost interest in school and dropped out." The couple began to hate each other, each accusing the other of failing to attain the highest cultivation level, and eventually divorced. Distraught with the family discord, Tian's aged father passed away in November 2000.[9]

In effect, Xinhua's account implied that Falun Gong had been indirectly responsible for the old man's death. In other cases, the sect is held to be directly culpable for the deaths of alleged followers. In a luncheon speech at the National Press Club on July 24, 2001, PRC ambassador to the United States Yang Jiechi maintained that many Falun Gong followers died from untreated illnesses because sect leaders had instructed them to shun medical treatment and assured them that should they die, they "will go to the heaven and fulfill their dreams."[10] According to Chinese government accounts, sect adherents who became grievously ill or died from untreated ailments included the following:

- Zhang Zhendong, a retired worker in Jilin province, studied Falun Gong's "scriptures" in the evening and worshipped Li's portrait at home. In May 1998, despite being convinced that "he would not die because Li Hongzhi was blessing him," Zhang was stricken with a dangerously high fever that persisted for more than one month.

- Liu Wenyong, a fifteen-year-old boy from Tianjin, contracted a "minor skin disease" in early 1999. Instead of seeking medical treatment, his mother sought to cure him with Falun Gong, which led his skin disease to "develop" into cancer.

- The wife of Wang Liyun, a former Falun Gong official from Hunan province, refused to take medication for an acute pain in her abdomen, believing that Falun Gong could cure any illness. On January 1, 1998, she was rushed to the hospital where she soon died of cancer. Only then did her husband become convinced of Li Hongzhi's "evil motives."

- Zhang Yanjie, a farmer in Henan province, began practicing Falun Gong in 1998. Although he suffered from coronary heart disease, he threw away his medicines and instead worshipped Li Hongzhi's portrait. On May 17, 1999, he felt "very bad in the heart" while practicing and died on his way to the hospital.

- Some twenty-three practitioners in Jilin, the northeastern province where the sect had originated, also died from untreated illnesses.[11]

More tragic still were those believers whose zeal led them to take their own lives. Among them were six Falun Gong adherents in

Jilin, one of whom was Zhang Xinghua, a thirty-two-year-old farmer who became a practitioner in 1996. As recounted by Xinhua, on January 14, 1997, believing that he had reached the highest level of cultivation, Zhang decided to test his immortality by leaping into the flames of a nearby boiler house. When the boilerkeepers prevented him from jumping into the boiler, he went to the top of the chimney and leapt. Severely wounded from the fall, he immediately lost consciousness. Instead of taking him to the hospital, his wife brought him home and, kneeling before a portrait of Li Hongzhi, implored the master to save her husband. Her prayers were ineffective as "Zhang died anyhow."[12]

Other alleged suicides included the following:

- Ma Jianmin, a retired worker from the Huabei oil field in northern China, who "cut his abdomen with a pair of scissors" to look for the law wheel he believed to be rotating inside.

- Gao Encheng, a leader of a Falun Gong practice group in the city of Chongqing, who, convinced of his immortality, jumped off a building holding his son in his arms.

- Long Gang, a self-employed small businessman in Chongqing, jumped off a bridge on the morning of July 17, 1999, holding his six-year-old son while murmuring Falun Gong instructions. The boy was saved by neighbors, but Long drowned.

- Liu Pinqing, a senior agronomist and recipient of an award from the Ministry of Agriculture, attempted self-immolation on February 4, 1999. A second suicide attempt in April was successful when Liu leapt into and drowned in a well.

- A Falun Gong practitioner in Jilin province who, on April 5, 2000, burnt himself to death.

- A nineteen-year-old college student and a twelve-year-old girl who, "bewitched" by the sect, died from their self-immolation in Tiananmen Square on January 23, 2001.[13]

More egregious still were the murders allegedly committed by Falun Gong adherents of individuals they believed to be demons. Beijing directly attributed the homicides to Li Hongzhi's assertion that "devils are anywhere" and "humankind has become completely devil-like abnormal beings." The alleged murders included the following:

- Dong, a Falun Gong follower, who took a small knife and broke into the house of his neighbor Jiang Wencai, a seventy-six-year-old retiree, and stabbed the latter in the neck.

- Yuan Tianyun of Guangdong province, "a good girl who studied hard at school," broke into the home of a neighbor. Believing that the man was among those who had "insulted" her in her dreams, Yuan killed him with a knife.

- Wang Xuezhong, a young man "addicted to the cult," accused his father of being a devil and stabbed him seventeen times in the head, neck, and chest area on August 23, 1996. His father later died from the injuries.

- Wu Deqiao, a thirty-six-year-old clerk with the Wujiang supply and marketing cooperative in Jiangsu province, "chopped his wife to death with a kitchen knife" in

February 1998 because "she tried to stop him from practicing."

- Li Ting, a graduate student and Falun Gong follower in Hebei province who, convinced that his parents were demons, killed them with a knife on March 20, 1999. When asked by the police why he killed his parents, the young man answered, "I think they are devils and I am a Buddha, so I have to wipe them out."

- Twenty-nine-year-old Qiu Defeng, a practitioner from Haikou, Hainan, axed his sixty-eight-year-old uncle to death on December 11, 2001. His uncle was like a father to Qiu, having brought him up and financing his university education. Qiu, suspecting that his uncle was plotting to murder him, hacked him to death with a kitchen knife. Later, Qiu reportedly denounced the sect for destroying his trust in people, including his uncle, and leading him "to commit such an appalling act."[14]

Altogether, according to the Chinese government in July 2001, whether it was by disease, suicide, or murder, Falun Gong, "bearing every feature of a cult," was responsible for more than 1,660 deaths in China.[15]

Harmful to Society

More than harming the health and lives of people, Beijing maintains that Falun Gong's "illegal" activities had also "seriously disrupted public order." To begin with, according to a senior PRC Ministry of Public Security officer, the sect "used the Internet to spread rumors . . . which has created disturbances for the government and disrupted social stability."[16]

More than that, the sect had also hurt society by preventing government and other institutions from doing their work. As an example, in May 1998, more than 1,000 Falun Gong devotees surrounded a television station in Beijing to protest being labeled a "cult." They succeeded in forcing the station to telecast a more favorable program. The following year, in April, sect activists again disrupted social order when they objected to physicist He Zuoxiu writing that Falun Gong was a "superstitious cult" and health hazard. When the magazine that carried He's article refused to issue a written apology, some 6,000 believers protested before the editorial office in Tianjin. When one of them was forcibly removed by the police, the protesters went to the municipal government. The alleged beating and arrest of ten protesters instigated the massive demonstration before the Communist Party compound in Beijing the next day.

If the accusations of having harmed the well-being of people and society are not enough, Beijing also imputes to Falun Gong a variety of other failings. Those shortcomings range from the relatively minor to egregious crimes of treason and sedition.

Superstitious and Antiscience

The sect has been denounced for promoting unscientific ideas of "idealism, theism and feudal superstition," including the assertion that the earth had undergone many prehistoric civilizations, that botanical plants have consciousness, that there are multiple universes, and that the end days are imminent. As one PRC writer put it: "Extraordinary claims"—such as those espoused by Li Hong-zhi—"require extraordinarily rigorous confirming evidence," which Li has failed to provide.[17]

Beijing attributes those unscientific assertions to Li's shallow and erroneous understanding of science, an understanding that is described as that of a grade school student. As an example, Li erroneously claimed that human eyesight is governed by the pineal gland. More than being unscientific, Li evinces an antipathy and hostility toward science when he dismisses science as being ignorant of the real truths about the universe, which, he claims, only he knows. This is why, Li insisted, "the world should listen to him, otherwise everything will be lost."[18]

Hypocritical

Beijing also criticizes Falun Gong for being sanctimonious. Specifically, the sect and its leader are accused of not being true to their professed virtues of truthfulness, benevolence, and tolerance. Instead of being truthful, they are duplicitous and fraudulent; instead of benevolent, they are uncaring; instead of tolerant, they are rigid and fanatical. All of which, according to Beijing, makes Falun Gong and its leader outright hypocrites.

To begin with, although Li preached the virtue of truthfulness, the Chinese government asserts that he used fraud to enrich himself and his family by selling books as well as audio and video products. For example, in 1995, Li and his followers made nearly $12,000 (100,000 yuan) from the sale of just one book; sales of audiotapes and videotapes of his lectures generated another $36,000 (300,000 yuan). Another $240,000 (2 million yuan) came from organizing Falun Gong study classes in two cities, Beijing and Changchun. Former sect members in the Inner Mongolia Autonomous Region also claimed that the sect had swindled a large amount of money from its practitioners in a pyramid scheme. Li's fraudulent activities were so lucrative that, in just one day—May 4, 1994—he reaped $14,000. As the Policy and Law and Regulations Department of the PRC's State Press and Publication Administration put it, Falun Gong confused right and wrong and has "deceived . . . a lot of people."[19]

As evidence of his ill-gotten wealth from "cheating practitioners and other benefactors," the public security police of Li's native Jilin province cited the following:

- A $14,000 (116,000 yuan) "luxury house" in Changchun, capital of Li's native Jilin province, which he purchased in 1994.

- A second house that was under construction in the same city.

- Expensive furniture, electronics, and personal items, including a twenty-nine-inch Sony color television, a set of "super acoustic equipment," a genuine leather "luxury" sofa, seven "high-quality" watches, and "modern office facilities."

- Plans to erect a Falun Research Center in Huailai County in Hebei province on sixty hectares of land.

- The enjoyment of a "luxurious life" by Li and his family in the United States.[20]

Nor is Falun Gong true to its second virtue of benevolence. Instead of being compassionate, Li Hongzhi is disapproving of homosexuals. More than that, it is claimed that sect members are not benevolent toward each other, not to speak of strangers. An example of their indifference was the treatment accorded Liu Renfang, a fifty-two-year-old farmer from Sichuan province and a practitioner since 1998 who refused to seek medical help for her persistent headaches and tracheitis. In December 2000, Liu and five other sect adherents went to Beijing, intent on defying the government's ban by assembling in Tiananmen Square on New Year's Day. On December 18, however, half a month before the planned demonstration, she suddenly died. According to a Xinhua account, her companions "were so brutal that they neglected her death and just put her body into a smelly sewer in order to destroy the evidence." All of which constitutes "irrefutable evidence" of the "anti-human nature" of the "notorious Falun Gong cult."[21]

As for the third virtue of tolerance, Beijing observed that although Li Hongzhi pays lip service to the importance of forbearance, in actuality he "cannot stand any criticism or alternative views." Whenever Falun Gong or its leader is criticized, Li "gets his followers to create a disturbance."[22] Indeed, in 1998 and 1999, believers did react to criticisms by protesting before a television station, a magazine's editorial office, the Tianjin municipal government, and the Communist Party compound in Beijing.

Illegal and Criminal

More than being hypocritical, it is claimed that Falun Gong also violated China's laws and as a consequence is an illicit organization. To begin with, in contravention of the government's requirement, none of the sect's many branches in China is registered with the authorities, which makes Falun Gong's very existence in China illicit. Given that, it stands to reason that the sect is also in violation of other laws. Among them are nothing less than China's national constitution, as well as "civil, criminal, and tax codes, and regulations for organizations, publishing, assemblies, parades, and demonstrations."[23]

In effect, not only is the sect's very existence unlawful, it was also "involved in many illegal activities," according to the Policy and Law and Regulations Department (PLRD) of China's State Press and Publication Administration. Chief among those activities was the massive demonstration in Beijing on April 25, 1999. It was that event that alerted party leaders to the realization that instead of being "a simple problem," the sect is nothing less than a threat to China and its government. Not only does Beijing accuse the sect of planning to overthrow Communist Party rule, it claims that the sect has the active assistance and support of foreign governments and international groups hostile to China.[24]

Treasonous

On October 25, 1999, China's Ministry of Public Security accused sect adherents of having stolen some fifty-nine classified state documents, twenty of which were allegedly top secret. To make matters worse, ten of the classified documents were leaked by adherents to "anti-China" overseas individuals and organizations that included international human rights organizations, "the Dalai Lama clique," and foreign governments, especially those in the West. As *China Daily* put it, to foment instability and break up China, anti-China groups and forces had provided Falun Gong with their uncritical sympathy and support because they "don't want to see a strong China or a China with a stable environment for economic development."[25]

As examples of the support given by anti-China forces to Falun Gong, Beijing cited the following: Amnesty International's declaration in October 1999 of its support for the sect; the U.S. immigration authorities' granting of political asylum to a Falun Gong follower in November 1999; and Washington's statement of concern on December 6, 1999, concerning Beijing's banning of the sect. In effect, according to Beijing, Li Hongzhi is more than the leader of an evil cult—he and his sect are "a pawn of international anti-China forces" and, as such, have committed treason by aiding and abetting the enemies of China.[26]

Seditious

More than being a pawn of foreign forces, Falun Gong had worked directly against the government. In the words of Ambassador Yang

Jiechi, "Some people say the issue touches religious freedom. [But] Falun Gong [itself] has said time and again that it is not a religion. I believe Falun Gong has an ulterior motive." That motive, according to a commentary in the *People's Daily* of October 10, 2000, is none other than "to overturn the People's Republic of China and to subvert the socialist system."[27]

Beijing asserted that the sect sought to accomplish its "ulterior motive" by instilling doubt and distrust and thus alienating people from the authorities. Adherents were persuaded to disengage and detach themselves from society by surrendering "their ideals and pursuits, and eschew[ing] social practice." In this manner, the potential contribution of otherwise productively engaged citizens was siphoned from "the building of socialism with Chinese characteristics."[28]

To advance his "wicked" and "viperous" political ambitions, Li also systematically manipulated and exploited people's fears. By preaching that social problems have become so numerous and intractable in the supposed end days that they defy political solution, he greatly eroded popular confidence in government, creating in them strong antigovernment and antisocial sentiments. Furthermore, by portraying the authorities as ineffectual, Li was actually promoting himself as the new leader. With his "doomsday idea," he both created and preyed on people's fears and desperation so that they would turn to him for salvation. After overthrowing the Communist Party state, his disciples would then install a new "so-called 'Falun world'" with Li as ruler.[29] As an article in the *People's Daily* of July 28, 1999, put it:

> Li Hongzhi's malicious fallacies in his doomsday message
> come from political motives. . . . Li Hongzhi preached that
> the earth will explode and that doomsday is coming and
> that no government can solve the problem and that only he

is the proper ruler of the world, which cannot do without
him. His purpose is crystal clear. . . . He deceived a lot of
people by deifying himself with the aim of taking the place
of the government and rule the world. . . . Li Hongzhi has
the evil aim of developing Falun Gong into a political force
that can be used against the government and Party.[30]

Under the guise of spiritual practice, Li had created an organized network of teaching centers and instruction stations that coor-
dinated millions of his followers in "secret activities." As their master, he used his control over his disciples to "instigate" them to
attack the media and government institutions, as well as organize
large-scale "illegal gatherings" to put pressure on the authorities.
The largest of those gatherings was the one on April 25, 1999,
when more than 10,000 believers surrounded the Communist Party
compound. All of which, according to Beijing, amounted to nothing less than a vast "backyard conspiracy."[31]

Well Organized

Any political movement that aims to overthrow the state must be
well organized. It is argued that is precisely the case with Falun
Gong. Contrary to the sect's denial, Beijing insists Falun Gong was
intricately and well organized.

Chongqing was representative of Falun Gong's complex network in China. In that city, the sect was hierarchically organized into
five layers. At the top was the general station, below which were
subbranches, followed by first-level and second-level instruction
centers, and at the lowest level were numerous exercise centers
where adherents flocked for their collective exercises. The Chinese
government claimed that the head of the Chongqing general station
had been personally selected by Li Hongzhi via a letter of appoint-

ment. Li's appointee, in turn, chose two deputies as assistants. The general station had three subbranches, each with a director and an executive deputy director. Below the subbranches were 56 first- and second-level instruction centers, and 890 exercise centers, each with its own leaders. Altogether, 358 individuals occupied leadership roles in the five layers of organization, people whom Beijing identifies as the "core organizers" and "behind-the-scene plotters."[32]

At the peak of the movement in 1998, thousands of Falun Gong tutors nationwide guided practitioners in exercise and study sessions in parks and plazas at dawn each day. The tutors were, in turn, grouped into stations that convened regularly to discuss the development of the sect and to plan periodic mass events. Station chiefs communicated with the sect's nerve center in China—the Falun Dafa Research Society (FDRS) in Beijing. In turn, FDRS took its orders directly from Li Hongzhi.[33]

This vertical nationwide organization enabled practitioners in Chongqing (and other cities) to act expeditiously in response to Master Li's directives. According to Beijing, beginning in 1998, practitioners were mobilized to besiege Chongqing's news media on numerous occasions. They allegedly received their instructions from Li who transmitted them through phone calls and faxes to the FDRS, and from there to the general station in Chongqing.[34]

The sect had a similar organization in China's other cities. According to Yu Ruichen, former head of the sect's general training center in Zhengzhou, Henan, Li Hongzhi "was lying when he said that the sect had no organizations. As a matter of fact, it had a strict organization system, with the Beijing-based Falun Dafa Research Society as its top governing body. It set up general training centers, substations and exercise spots in provinces and municipalities. Li's orders were passed down from the Beijing-based society to every practitioner through telephones, fax and the Internet."[35]

Jin Guiqin, an erstwhile leader of a training base in Anshan,

Liaoning, also attested that Falun Gong was well organized and that orders from above were relayed by phone, E-mail, and the Internet. Similarly, Feng Runti, another leader, confirmed that sect units were arranged hierarchically. Li's teachings and instructions were communicated to Feng's substation from higher levels; the substation, in turn, reported its operations to the station immediately above. Feng claimed that Li Hongzhi exerted his control over practitioners mainly through his ideology: "We were told that what he said was law, and whoever opposed his statements would be committing a felony."[36]

Such testimony indicates that Falun Gong was a "tightly run . . . highly organized illegal system." In addition to being well organized, it was intricate and complex—more than 1,500 constituent units made up the sect's presence in one province (Jilin) alone. According to Beijing, Falun Gong even succeeded in penetrating important party and government organizations.[37] As the Xinhua News Agency put it,

> Falun Gong has said that it doesn't have any organization and that it is managed in a loose way, but the evidence gathered by public security departments . . . shows the opposite to be true. It also shows that every Falun Gong branch has an organization with propaganda, training, organization, and administrative sections, each with a clear duty. These branches cooperate and communicate in a way that helped Falun Gong expand in such a short period of time. . . . [Additionally,] Falun Gong also has reserve forces, whose purpose is to avoid investigation by public security departments and to continue the illegal activities.[38]

Altogether, according to Beijing, Falun Gong had a "virtual" organization in China composed of 39 provincial branches, 1,900 lower-level "guidance stations," and 23,000 practice sites. The sect also maintained 40 international Web sites—in China, the United States, Hong Kong, and Taiwan.[39]

For Beijing, the massive demonstration on April 25, 1999, both illustrated and confirmed the sect's organizational prowess. The protest was planned in large part via E-mail. According to one account, Li Hongzhi arrived in Beijing on April 22, on Northwest Airline flight 087 from the United States. Two days later, on April 24, he departed for Hong Kong, and from there he used long distance phone calls to "secretly orchestrate" the demonstration that took place the next day.[40]

As recounted by Xinhua, before he left Beijing, Li entrusted the implementation of his plan to two key aides, Li Chang and Wang Zhiwen. At 8:30 A.M. on April 24, the leaders of Beijing's general station and substations met at 7 Cangjingguan Lane in the eastern part of the city. The substation leaders were assigned the tasks of providing transportation and sanitation and maintaining order and security at the demonstration. Liu Zhichun, deputy director of the general station, was put in charge of all the substations in Beijing; Wang Zhiwen was responsible for the areas outside Beijing.[41]

That afternoon, the key organizers convened another meeting. A command headquarters and a liaison center were established. Two individuals were charged with communications between the gathering site and the headquarters; another was responsible for publishing "propaganda" on the Internet. After the meeting, Wang Zhiwen made numerous calls to local sect leaders in Tianjin and the provinces of Hebei, Shandong, and Liaoning, asking them to mobilize believers to go to Beijing the next morning "to protect Falun Dafa." To encourage turnout, the organizers disseminated a statement by Li Hongzhi, in which he urged his disciples to stand up to their responsibility of protecting the Great Law of the Wheel. At the same time, Li was punctilious in instructing his disciples that, should they proceed to Beijing, they were to do so voluntarily as individuals.[42]

No doubt this was to provide him with deniability in the event he was accused by the authorities of planning and organizing an unsanctioned public demonstration. What he did not anticipate, of course, is that none of this matters in the "rule of law" of the People's Republic of China.

Government Suppression as Necessary and Legitimate

In making its case against Falun Gong, the Chinese government has charged the sect and its leader with a panoply of offenses ranging from the trivial to egregious crimes of treason and sedition. At the same time, the government has consistently presented itself as irreproachable in its conduct toward the sect, ever insistent that it acted appropriately and legitimately. The government maintains that not only has it scrupulously abided by the rule of law in its campaign against Falun Gong, but it was motivated by the purest and best of intentions.

That intent, simply put, is to protect people and society from the depredations of iniquity, to "liberate" those who had "fallen" into an "evil cult." Deliverance entails that the sect's lies be exposed and the indoctrinated minds of followers be "thoroughly cleansed" to restore their self-confidence and humanity. But Falun Gong's offenses transcend that of being an evil cult; it had degenerated into "a virtual reactionary political force" that threatens the country, and as such, it must be destroyed. As *China Daily* put it, "history has proved time and again that persons who have become the enemies of the country, people and nation will be eventually doomed."[43]

Other than its interest in protecting people, Beijing also justifies its eradication of Falun Gong by asserting that it is required to do so by the rule of law. The main legal instrument that mandates the government's suppression of the sect is the Provisions on the Registration and Administration on Social Groups. These provisions both require and empower the Ministry of Civil Affairs to outlaw Falun Gong on July 22, 1999, on grounds that the latter had never registered with the ministry and, as a consequence, was an illegal entity. As such, whatever activities the sect undertook—especially those "disturbing social order or opposing the government"—were also illicit, as was any publicity of the sect.[44]

As if the provisions alone were inadequate for the task, Beijing further augmented its legal armory with an array of other laws and rules, including the following:

- Article 300 of the revised Criminal Law prohibiting and punishing "cult-related criminal activities." The law was revised by the national legislature, the National People's Congress (NPC), on March 14, 1997.

- The Law on Gatherings, Parades and Demonstrations, requiring the prior approval of the public securities authorities for any public assemblage.

- Administrative rules supplementing the law and issued by the Beijing municipal government against illegal gatherings, parades, demonstrations, and the posting of "illegal publicity material."

- The People's Armed Police Law empowering the police to question, disperse, and detain Falun Gong members found in "illegal" gatherings in Tiananmen Square.

- The Explanations on the Application of Law Concerning Crimes Involved in the Organization and Utilization of Cults, published on October 30, 1999, by the Supreme People's Court and the Supreme People's Procuratorate.

- A resolution passed by a special session of the NPC Standing Committee on October 30, 1999, restricting religious cults such as the already banned Falun Gong. The resolution also requires the courts, prosecutors, and police to control and subdue any cult activity. Severe penalties, including the death penalty, are provided for cult leaders.

- Another revision of the Criminal Law by the NPC in November 1999 formally designating Falun Gong as a "devil cult." Sect members are liable to prosecution for murder, fraud, endangering national security, and other crimes. Those convicted can be sentenced to longer prison terms than previously mandated by the criminal code for cultists.[45]

Last, but not the least, is the legal device used to incarcerate sect members in labor camps—the Transformation Through Labor System that was passed by the NPC Standing Committee on August 1, 1957, and supplemented by "additional related rules" approved by the same committee on November 29, 1979, and by a provisional regulation promulgated by the State Council in January 1982. Beijing's policy is to distinguish between ordinary and core Falun Gong members—"between those people who realized their mistakes and wish to correct them, and the diehards." It maintains that the majority of practitioners had been deceived by the cult and should be "reeducated" to free themselves from its spiritual shackles. Beijing insists that sect devotees who have been dispatched to labor camps for reeducation were not sent there because of their religious beliefs, but rather because they refused to break their ties with the cult, had "disturbed social order," or had committed "minor cult-related crimes." The immurement of cult members in reeducation camps must be approved by transformation-through-labor administrative commissions operating under provincial or municipal governments. Furthermore, Beijing asserts that those detained are protected by certain unspecified "Chinese laws" that safeguard their legal rights, including their personal rights; property rights; and the rights to sue, appeal, and communicate. Measures taken to preserve these rights include "reduction of sentences, home-based transformation and early release from the institutions."[46]

This arsenal of laws, rules, and regulations legitimized the sentencing by Beijing's Intermediate People's Court of four core Falun Gong leaders on December 26, 1999. Li Chang, Wang Zhiwen, Ji Liewu, and Yao Jie were given prison sentences ranging from seven to eighteen years for obstructing law enforcement and causing deaths through cult activities. Their sentencing was followed by the conviction of an unspecified number of sect members by local courts across China. Altogether, according to Beijing, "considering the size and scope of the cult, only a handful of Falun Gong members have been severely punished according to law." It is claimed that official statistics showed that, as of January 15, 2001, only 242 "backbone" sect members had been given criminal punishments throughout the country. Even in these cases, Beijing insisted, the individuals were punished not for their religious beliefs or practice, but for their violation of Chinese law.[47]

In effect, Beijing would have us believe that its judicial organs have been unimpeachable in their comportment toward the sect, having based their sentencing decisions on nothing but facts and laws. More than that, in suppressing Falun Gong, the government has acted no differently than its counterparts in other countries similarly besieged by dangerous cults, such as those in Japan and Uganda. As an official of the Information Office of China's State Council put it: "The government's ban and crackdowns on the Falun Gong cult have legal basis and are meant to safeguard social stability and protect people's life and property—which is the government's main responsibility. . . . A cult is a social cancer . . . [and] the government of any country that has experienced a cult should adopt a watchful and preventive attitude, and handle such groups with a firm hand."[48]

Beijing's irrefutable conduct toward Falun Gong extends to the treatment of those confined in labor camps. In May 2001, to quash international criticism of those camps, Beijing invited journalists from several countries to visit a particularly notorious labor camp near Shenyang, Liaoning—the Masanjia Reeducation-through-Labor Center. All the inmates in the center's Second Women's Unit were Falun Gong devotees, some of whom reportedly had been tortured and abused. The invited reporters included those from the Associated Press, NBC, and ABC; Japan's NHK; the Australian Broadcasting Corporation; and the Singapore Press Holdings.

Not surprisingly, the Chinese government vehemently denied mistreating the inmates. On the contrary, the government claimed that it was the center's success in rehabilitation that had made it "the most heavily attacked" target of Li Hongzhi and the sect's headquarters in New York. Claims that female inmates were tossed into cells full of male prisoners, beaten with electric batons, or sent to "water cells" or solitary confinement in dark rooms were "sheer fabrication." Contrary to those scurrilous accusations, the center treated its inmates as "sisters who went astray," victims of an evil cult. As an example of the center's compassionate treatment, the authorities offered Xia Yulan, a forty-nine-year-old inmate who was a former lecturer at a Communist Party school. When asked by one of the visiting reporters whether she had been beaten or tortured, Xia said "no" with a firm voice, adding that the "policewomen here are very kind to me, they care for my daily life and I am very grateful to them."[49]

The next month, in June 2001, another group of some twenty

reporters from Hong Kong, Macao, and Taiwan were invited to tour another labor camp—the Tuanhe Camp in the southern suburbs of Beijing. As described by *China Daily,* the camp resembled a country club more than a prison. Although the inmates had to attend compulsory lectures on the "rights and duty of a citizen," they lived in a bucolic compound surrounded with grass and trees. Some inmates were seen "maintaining the grounds, attending deers, rabbits and birds raised on the camp, some playing basketball." The camp claimed to have successfully reeducated more than 90 percent of its inmates. At the time of the visit, there were 340 Falun Gong "addicts" in custody. One of them, a twenty-three-year-old young man named Liu Yang assured the visiting reporters that the "police treat me like a friend here."[50]

Liu Yang is only one of many former Falun Gong followers who have been redeemed—"thanks to the government's help, many innocent people, especially women, children and the elderly were saved and have gone back to normal lives." Another example is Cai Shuliu of Shanghai, who was detained in 2000 for illegally distributing sect brochures. After the government helped her break away from the cult's psychological control, she realized what "a terrible mistake" she had made, "how silly" she had been, and how "Li Hongzhi took advantage of so many ordinary people for his own evil purposes." Similarly, Liu Lan, a self-employed businesswoman in Guangdong province, admitted that she had been "stupid" for believing in Falun Gong. Until she was reeducated by the government, she had been "living a nightmare."[51]

Cai and Liu are not alone. In July 2001, the Communist Party's Central Committee and the Ministry of Justice convened an anticult exhibition in Beijing. On display were hundreds of red flags presented by former Falun Gong practitioners and their families proclaiming their "gratitude for helping them out of that destructive lifestyle." The same month, some 110 former sect adherents wrote a letter to China's Ministry of Justice, expressing their appreciation to the ministry "for saving them from the clutches of the cult." They had been "brainwashed by cult leader Li Hongzhi's fallacious preaching." Happily, the government's reeducation program enabled them to see the error of their ways. Despite having come to their senses, however, the letter writers remained confined to a reeducation institution in the city of Tianjin.[52]

The Will of the People?

On January 15, 2001, one and a half years after the instigation of a nationwide campaign against Falun Gong—a campaign that reminded many of Mao Zedong's Cultural Revolution—a spokesman for the Chinese government justified the campaign by insisting that "it reflected the will of the majority of the Chinese people" who had demanded that action be taken against the sect. As evidence of the people's support, the authorities pointed to a scroll displayed in the July 2001 anti-cult exhibit in Beijing, bearing the signatures of more than a million citizens in support of the ban. In effect, Beijing contends that in suppressing the sect, it is simply responding to popular demand. As Ambassador Yang Jiechi put it, "If the overwhelming majority of the people in China consider Falun Gong as bad, one has to say that the banning of the cult represents 'the people's will,' rather than 'a conclusion imposed on the people by the government.' "[53]

But the reality is not quite as Beijing presents it.

In the first place, it is disingenuous for the Chinese government to aver that in suppressing the sect it was merely responding to the "people's will." Although economic liberalization since 1979 has transformed the country, China's political system remains unreformed and authoritarian. Today China still lacks the freedom of the press and of speech that can ensure that whatever popular opinion is formed among the populace is not simply a reflection of the will of the state. Instead of being a genuine expression of popular opinions and sentiments, the "people's will" that Beijing cited is the result of the systematic shaping, molding, and orchestration by the government's massive campaign against Falun Gong. Even if one were to grant the existence of a bona fide popular opinion against Falun Gong, it is still curious that a government campaign against an already reviled group would be needed in the first place, a campaign that included the two-week anti-cult exhibition in which photos, letters, videos, books, and other media were deployed to educate citizens on how to combat "this insidious problem."[54]

But that is not the only troubling aspect of Beijing's case against Falun Gong. For almost every one of its accusations against the sect, it can be argued that the Communist Party government has been equally, if not more, guilty. Furthermore, even if Beijing's accusations were valid, that does not justify its treatment of the believers, a treatment that included the arrest, imprisonment, and reported torture of thousands of citizens who had engaged in nothing more than the practice of health-promoting exercises and the belief, no matter how misguided, in the fantastic ideas of a new religion.

There are other questions still. If Falun Gong is as popularly loathed as Beijing portrays, why is the government pursuing the sect with such single-minded ruthlessness and determination? And if Falun Gong is as inane as Beijing maintains, what can account for its appeal to perhaps as many as 100 million believers? These questions will be explored in the next chapter.

Chapter Five
The Persecution of Other Faiths

It has been several years since the massive demonstration in Beijing by followers of Falun Gong. In the interim, tens of thousands of believers were imprisoned, "reeducated" in labor camps, committed to mental hospitals, detained in holding centers, or kept under surveillance by family members and employers. Many were tortured; an estimated 150 to 350 were killed. By whatever measure, the treatment inflicted on the faithful of this religious sect can only be described as brutal.

Beijing justifies its suppression of Falun Gong with a catalog of accusations: that the sect is an evil cult; that it harms people and society, being superstitious, antiscience, hypocritical, and treasonous; and that it has violated laws and aims at nothing less than the overthrow of the government. The problem is that there is little, if any, independent corroboration for these claims, China being a country where government remains the exclusive purview of the same party that has ruled since 1949. As a consequence, the judiciary is neither autonomous nor impartial, but is instead a pawn of the Chinese Communist Party. That is made evident in the preamble to the state constitution, which prescribes that the People's Republic of China is to be governed by "the leadership of the Communist Party"; similarly, the purpose of China's Criminal Law is "to use criminal punishments . . . to defend the system of the dictatorship of the proletariat," the proletariat being "represented" by the CCP.[1]

In such a political system, truth becomes hostage to the state. Not only are the people at the state's mercy, but ironically the government is also a victim because what it says lacks credibility, even if it is telling the truth. Given the compromised nature of the Chinese judiciary, Beijing's oft-stated claim that it has constructed a "rule of law" is unconvincing. To rationalize its mutated brand of socialism—one in which capitalists are invited to become Communist Party members—Beijing calls it a "socialism with Chinese characteristics." Similarly, the party conceals its arbitrary and dictatorial dominion over China by calling it a "rule of law." But the latter, though much trumpeted by Beijing, is more fiction than truth. It would seem that, in addition to "socialism with Chinese characteristics," the country also has a "rule of law with Chinese characteristics." Instead of a system governed by law, the case of Falun Gong points to a country that, at best, has the form but neither the spirit nor substance of a rule of law.

Rule of Law with Chinese Characteristics

To begin with, the official directives and legal documents that Beijing employs against Falun Gong are contrary to both the Chinese constitution as well as international norms. Article 36 of the constitution states: "citizens enjoy freedom of religious belief. No state organ, public organization, or individual may compel citizens to believe in, or not to believe in, any religion; nor may they discriminate against citizens who believe in, or do not believe in, any religion." At the same time as it promises religious liberty, however, the constitution takes it away with the Orwellian Article 51, which stipulates that "the exercise by citizens of the People's Republic of China of their freedoms and rights may not infringe upon the interests of the state, of society and of the collective."[2] And in China's single-party state, the CCP determines the interests of the state, of society, and of the collective, as well as what constitutes an infringement of those interests.

As for international standards governing freedom of expression, association, and belief, although some restrictions are allowed, that does not mean that governments have carte blanche discretion to define for themselves the circumstances under which those liberties can be abridged. On the contrary, limits on civil and political rights must satisfy certain conditions: they must be provided by law; they must be necessary; they must be in pursuance of a legitimate objective, such as the protection of national security, public order, public health or morals; and they must be proportional to the provocation. Additionally, only those individuals found to be guilty of real crimes should be punished, not entire groups banned and hounded. And if religious freedom is circumscribed to protect public security, the constraints must be in direct proportion to the specific threat—and no more. In effect, whatever limitations are imposed on freedom of expression, association, and belief must be narrowly applied and specifically targeted so that they do not entirely undermine the people's exercise of their fundamental rights. To put it simply, such conditions and precautions are meant to ensure that abridgements are not deployed *simply* to suppress an opinion or belief.[3]

But that is exactly the purpose of Beijing's crackdown on Falun Gong and other so-called cults. Although international norms obligate the Chinese government to demonstrate why particular restrictions are necessary and why punishing members of Falun Gong and other groups is warranted, it has so far failed to do so.[4] There are also other problems, one of which is Beijing's penchant for retroactive legislation.

The CCP government seems to have convinced itself that instituting laws is all that is required for China to have a rule of law. But it takes more than the existence of laws to make a rule of law; these laws must be approved by a duly constituted authority. In China's case, the main legislative body is ostensibly the National People's Congress (NPC). But there are problems with both its putative law-making function and its representativeness.

To begin with, the NPC is at best an implausible legislative body for the simple reason that it meets once a year for only a week. No bona fide synod can complete its law-making tasks in such a short time, least of all the legislature for a country as populous as China, with one-fifth of the world's population. Additionally, the NPC's representativeness is questionable in that its 3,000-plus delegates have not been elected by the masses but were chosen by members of the provincial and autonomous-regional People's Congresses (PCs), which in turn had been selected by the delegates of the county and village-township People's Congresses. The entire system of congresses—from the national down to the village-township PCs—forms a pyramid of *indirect* election and representation in which popular participation occurs only at the lowest tier when ordinary people vote to select the delegates to the village-township PCs. Even here, the representativeness of the delegates is doubtful. To be eligible as candidates, individuals must either be approved by the Communist Party or nominated by ten or more PC members, a process that effectively ensures that only the politically orthodox survive the arduous screening process. As the culmination of this process, the National People's Congress is a parliament more in name than in substance. The reality is that despite a marginal increase in recent years of dissenting votes, the NPC remains a rubber-stamp body for decisions that have already been made by the leaders of the Communist Party.[5]

Exacerbating an already problematic legal system is the Chinese government's penchant for ex post facto legislation. For example, Beijing banned Falun Gong on July 22, 1999, but the law authorizing such a ban, the anti-cult law, was not approved by the NPC until three months later in October. More than that, long before the government began suppressing Falun Gong, the persecution of other religious and quasi-religious groups was already underway. This was the "antisuperstition" campaign in which leaders of such groups were detained, assigned without trial to labor camps, or tried under a variety of criminal charges, all without benefit of law. In the case of one group, the Spirit Church (Lingling Jiao), Beijing began hounding it in the early 1990s, several years before the NPC passed the anti-cult law.[6]

Adding to the problem of retroactive laws is the unfairness of the trials of alleged core members of Falun Gong. In a country where 99 percent of trials bring a guilty verdict, most trials are closed to the public, with some being held in secret. In the case of Falun Gong, the judicial process was prejudiced from the outset against the defendants. Instead of innocence until proven otherwise, there was a presumption of guilt. Nor did the state provide any evidence that the defendants had been involved in activities that could rightly be regarded as crimes under international standards.[7]

Adding to the problems of retroactive legislation and unfair trials are the thousands of Falun Gong faithful who were not even accorded a trial but were arbitrarily dispatched to labor camps at the discretion of local "public security" officers. Today, in the People's Republic, the government's executive branch—in the persons of the police—can impose administrative sanctions on anyone without benefit of judicial review, effectively bypassing the entire judicial system. Through the Security Administrative Punishment Act, the local constabulary can independently issue warnings, impose fines, confiscate property, and detain individuals for up to fifteen days; through the 1979 Reeducation Through Labor Act, individuals can be imprisoned for one to three years, after which their incarceration can be extended for another year solely at the discretion of local officials.[8]

Yet another problem is the dubious authenticity of the denunciations made by former Falun Gong practitioners because of the government's carrot-and-stick approach to encourage and induce the condemnation. Promises are made to the practitioners that they would escape punishment if they complied with the authorities; if that failed to elicit the desired response, the practitioners would be threatened with detention, fines, and other penalties. As for those who allegedly died from illnesses because their faith in Falun Gong caused them to refuse medical treatment, such reports cannot be independently verified. Not only is the impartiality of the government's information doubtful, the burden of proof is on the state to establish a direct connection between the alleged deaths and the Falun Gong leadership, which Beijing has failed to do.[9]

The most egregious violation of the rule of law may be the government's use of torture against followers of Falun Gong and other cults, in violation of international norms and conventions. The available evidence indicates that detained Falun Gong adherents were subjected to abuse and ill treatment, their confessions regularly extracted through intimidation, sleep deprivation, and beatings. Some died in police custody in clouded circumstances, reportedly from torture. Women in particular seemed to have been singled out for torment, some with electric cattle prods. All of which led Amnesty International to conclude that the campaign against Falun Gong is politically motivated and that the legislation

employed in the crackdown is intended to convict people on politically driven charges and to further curb the fundamental freedoms
of the Chinese people.[10]

It Takes a Cult to Know a Cult

Even if Beijing's allegations against Falun Gong were true, the irony
is that the Chinese Communist Party is equally, if not more, guilty of
those same charges. Psychologist Carl Jung once maintained that
human beings are prone to deny and suppress that part of ourselves
that we believe to be weak, immoral, or defective. He called it our
"shadow." According to Jung, one way to deny our shadow—
thereby deluding ourselves that we are virtuous and perfect—is to
project it onto others through the mechanism of scapegoating.[11]
That seems to be what the Chinese government has done.

To begin with, by its own definition of "evil cult," the CCP
qualifies as one. According to that definition, a cult is a group that
"idolizes" a leader "who claims to be god . . . [and] brainwashes
believers," insisting that they "renounce all other beliefs to worship and obey him in transforming themselves into new men and
women." All of which causes believers "to lose their reason, dignity,
ability to distinguish right from wrong, becoming mentally deranged, commit suicide or murder, [and] attack party and government institutions." This definition would appear to be descriptive
of Maoist China.[12]

In the twenty-seven years when Mao Zedong ruled as a demigod, his every word and thought were the people's command as
they were urged to transform themselves into new socialist men and
women. During the Cultural Revolution period (1966–76) in particular, the adulation of Chairman Mao reached new heights. He
was revered as the "Great Helmsman" and the "never-setting red
sun" in the people's hearts; the little red book that contained his

aphorisms became their holy scripture. Goaded on by his vague exhortation to destroy old ideas and culture, the Chinese masses were whipped into a frenzy of recrimination and destruction. Schools and universities were closed, all the better to allow young people to form bands of Red Guards that roamed the country, laying waste to life and property. "Enemies of the people" were subjected to public vilification and abuse; in some areas, the vengeful masses took to cannibalizing their imagined adversaries.[13]

By the time Mao died in 1976, the People's Republic had managed to achieve the dubious distinction of having exacted the greatest human toll among communist countries—at 45 to 72 million. According to *The Black Book of Communism,* the deaths included the following: 6 to 10 million who were killed by the CCP before it came to power in 1949 (excluding those who died in the civil war with the Chinese Nationalists); 20 to 43 million who died between 1951 and 1961 from land reform and the Great Leap Forward; 1 to 3 million who lost their lives in the madness of the Cultural Revolution; perhaps 20 million "counterrevolutionaries" who perished in prisons and labor camps; as well as 10 to 20 percent of the inhabitants of Tibet who were killed in their failed uprising of 1959.[14] Together with the millions who languished in reeducation-through-labor camps, who were tortured and abused by Red Guards or "sent down" to the countryside to "learn" from the peasants, the population of China probably suffered more death, privation, and politically engineered devastation than any time in its history.

Not only did Mao's rule conform to Beijing's criterial attributes of an evil cult, it was also superstitious and antiscience and demonstrably harmful to people and society, indictments that Beijing has made against Falun Gong. Even after his death, the CCP refrained from renouncing Mao. On the contrary, when the party in 1979 undertook a review of its performance of the past thirty years, it concluded that despite "some mistakes" made by the Chairman, the preponderance (70 percent) of his tenure had been correct and laudable. The Chinese Communist Party's affirmation of Mao stands in marked contrast to its Soviet counterpart, which, in 1956 under Nikita Khrushchev, condemned Joseph Stalin for his reign of terror (1923–53).

More significantly still, the CCP's infliction of harm on the Chinese people did not end with Mao's death. Although the number and frequency of persecution have decreased since the days of Mao, today Christians and labor union activists are still persecuted, political dissidents are still imprisoned, Tibet remains a police state, and nameless multitudes still languish in prison camps.[15] Although the Chinese people enjoy greater freedoms in their daily lives, the CCP does not hesitate to bring all the brutal power of the state against any who step beyond its confines of tolerance, no matter how trivial the offense. An example is the arrest in March 1998 of a construction engineer, Liu Kangxiu, for writing an *unpublished* book advocating political reform. As Nicholas Kristof of the *New York Times* put it, "China is in many ways freer than it has ever been, and it's easy to be dazzled by the cellphones and skyscrapers. But alongside all that sparkles is the old police state." Citing secret CCP documents recently published in a book, *China's New Rulers,* Kristof reminded those prone to viewing China through rose-colored glasses that the country accounts for 97 percent of the world's executions, and that 15,000 Chinese are killed each year, either executed or shot by police while fleeing.[16]

More than that, the Communist Party is also "hypocritical"— another accusation it has made against Falun Gong. Deng Xiaoping, China's de facto leader from 1979 until his death in 1997, justified the Communist Party's continuing monopoly of political power by invoking the hoary notion of the party as vanguard. According to him, despite the many mistakes made by his party, especially the disastrous Cultural Revolution, it deserved to rule because its members were supposedly uniquely possessed of special moral virtues. They were selfless beings who worked only for the good of the people, neither exploiting the labor of others nor imposing their will by decree. They kept in close contact with the masses, representing their will and interests and inspiring their enthusiasm. Furthermore, CCP members spoke only the truth and opposed falsehood, and they clearly distinguished public from private interests, refraining from seeking personal favors and appointing people on merit alone.[17]

The problem is that these claims to virtue—on which the Communist Party still stakes its right to rule—are a hollow pretension. Its leaders have admitted as much as they repeatedly decry the pandemic corruption of party and government officials, against which the successive campaigns at eradication have proven ineffective. Instead, all indications are that graft has reached unprecedented levels. It is estimated that corruption may be costing the Chinese economy 4 percent of its gross domestic product (GDP) each year.[18] Other estimates put the figure much higher—at 13 to 15 percent of the GDP, totalling $150 billion in the past ten years.

Social Roots of Falun Gong and Other Cults

Contrary to Beijing's depiction, the general view of the international community is that instead of being an evil cult, Falun Gong is quite innocuous as sects go. More than being benign, the sect had served a useful social function that, at one time, was acknowledged by China's leaders. One believer described its ameliorative effects as follows: "The exercises got your circulation going, and meditation afterward helped dissipate frustrations from work and your crowded apartment block. China began to seem livable again."[19]

Although some of the sect's ideas variously may seem "weird," "cranky," "incredible," or "bizarre" to outsiders, by and large, its followers are taught to be good people and to uphold high moral standards.[20] Falun Gong undoubtedly has its share of charlatans and crooks, but it is neither sinister nor subversive as some sects clearly are. In the last analysis, it is better to spin law wheels in stomachs, as Falun Gong claims to do, than to brainwash the faithful, cheat them out of their life savings, or, as in the case of Japan's Aum Shinrikyo, attempt mass murder.

Toward a relatively harmless religious group such as Falun Gong, most countries—at least those in the West—would give its leader a street corner and a soapbox and let him have his say. Indeed, Western governments have been reflexively sympathetic with the sect.[21] It is a sign of Beijing's deep insecurity that it considers Falun Gong, or any group that may excite interest or allegiance outside the Communist Party, to be a major threat. Dissident Harry Wu explains that the regime is so feeble that it does not want people organized for even the most frivolous reason because although it may be a group of matchbox hobbyists today, tomorrow "you may turn your group to another purpose." Recalling an old saying, "You see a rope and fear it is a snake," Justin Yu, a Chinese journalist working in New York, similarly observes that the Communist Party is so paranoid and nervous that "if the wind blows . . . they imagine that a whole army is coming to destroy them."[22]

What Beijing fears is not so much Falun Gong itself, but what it represents—the underlying problems and instability in Chinese society. In effect, Beijing's persecution of Falun Gong goes beyond issues of human rights violations, which are grave and fully deserving of the international community's concern, and raises troubling questions concerning conditions in China today.

Historically, secret societies and millenarian movements tended to arise in China during times of great social upheaval and psychohistorical dislocation. Today it is no different. That a set of beliefs as fantastic as those of Falun Gong can capture the allegiance of perhaps as many as 100 million people—most of whom are members of the educated middle class, including some from the party, military, and government—speaks to the presence of a profound malaise in Chinese society. A Chinese government official admitted as much. Citing political corruption and widespread discontent among farmers and workers who had not profited from the economic reforms, the anonymous official lamented, "China has so many social problems." According to him, the government's plan is to keep the disaffected groups apart because "if they link up and there's a major disaster, it will be like throwing a spark on a pile of dry tinder."[23]

The "dry tinder" is made up of the many groups that are marginalized and alienated in the midst of China's economic boom. Among them are the elderly and the unemployed who figure so prominently in Falun Gong's ranks. In the urban areas, there are the retirees and state employees who must make do on fixed incomes at a time when state medical and other welfare benefits are disappearing. Not surprisingly, they are precisely those who find solace in the sect's salvific promise of health and enlightenment. As one Beijing academic puts it, "If medicines and doctors were not so expensive . . . most of these people would never even think of trying the Falun Gong."[24]

According to Beijing, China's urban unemployment rate stood at 3.3 percent (or 6.19 million people) at the end of June 2001. But many analysts, including PRC Labor Minister Zhang Zuoji, believed that figure to be a gross underestimation; not only does it leave out rural unemployment, it also excludes the hidden urban unemployment of about 6 million laid-off workers from the state-owned enterprises (SOE) who were kept on payrolls at token salaries.[25] To keep unemployment from rising further, China will have to maintain a minimum economic growth rate of 7 percent, which was a major reason motivating China to seek membership in the World Trade Organization (WTO).

Among China's other marginalized groups are the 80 million or so active workers in the dysfunctional SOEs, and the 800–900 million peasants who still comprise the majority (two-thirds) of China's population. Spontaneous labor protests have steadily increased in recent years, from 60,000 cases in 1998 to 100,000 in 1999. An example was the demonstration in March 2002 of some 5,000 workers of China's largest oil field in Daqing.[26]

The peasants, for their part, increasingly chafe under a stagnant rural economy made worse by usurious taxes and fees. Cao Jinqing, PRC scholar and author of *China Along the Yellow River,* maintains that away from the country's thriving coastal regions and cities, a vast swath of the interior lives in stagnation. Although Beijing has repeatedly called on local officials to reduce rural taxes and fees, the central government still does not provide the funding needed for public services in the countryside. Local officials, as a consequence, turn to imposing an array of special taxes as solution. Many local governments also inflate earnings figures, which are used as a basis for yet more taxes. In Hubei province, as an example, farmers were asked to pay taxes equivalent to 50 percent of their net income. Many became so desperate that they sought recourse in suicide: in one month (September 2001), twenty-six peasants across the country took their own lives because they could not pay the taxes demanded by local cadres.[27]

All of which provoked thousands of peasants across China to undertake the protests and demonstrations that have become widespread in recent years. Reports of up to 20,000 protesters blocking major roads or railways are not uncommon. Some demonstrations end only after violent clashes with police. An example was the protest by a thousand farmers against alleged corruption in a village in Guangdong province on July 30, 2001, which ended only when more than 450 policemen were brought in to quell the unrest. State media often carry reports of powerful local officials hiring thugs to beat or even kill protesting farmers; officials also misuse their power to have protesters arrested and imprisoned.[28]

The plight of the workers and peasants has not escaped the notice of the central government, nor are its leaders unaware of the dangers inherent in their predicament. None other than President Jiang Zemin in February 2002 emphasized that the country's stability hinged on giving poor workers and farmers more of the benefits of economic growth. Cao Jinqing is even blunter. Noting the irony that the "Communist Party came to power to overthrow the landlords" but now "has become the new landlord," he warned that if the condition of the Chinese peasantry is not improved, today's small-scale rebellions of several thousands will soon grow into a bigger crisis.[29]

That "bigger crisis" may well come about as a result of China's being admitted into the WTO in December 2001, which brings with it increasing foreign competition. Labor Minister Zhang Zuoji expected workers to be laid off in sectors ranging from farming to banking. Chinese farmers, in particular, will be affected. Most of them own small plots that cannot come close to achieving the economies of scale of modern Western farms. In the five years following its admission into the WTO, China will have to lift its bans on imports of foreign wheat and meat, as well as reduce its tariffs on agricultural commodities from 31 percent to an average of 17 percent. The average duty on key U.S. agricultural exports will decrease even more—to 14 percent. Entry into the WTO therefore opened the floodgates to a mass of new agricultural products, giving China's farmers a five-year scramble to shift from growing low-value grains to higher-value fruits and vegetables. Even without foreign competition, real farm incomes in China have been lackluster for some time, their rate of growth falling for four consecutive years to 2.1 percent in 2000 from an average annual growth rate of 6 percent in the early 1990s. Without a government statistical gloss, the figures may be even worse. In the inland provinces, some 650 million peasants saw their incomes rise by less than a dollar a year between 1985 and 1997.[30]

It seems inevitable that as WTO membership opens China's doors to overseas agricultural imports, millions more will be fleeing the countryside for the cities and coastal regions in search of work. They will swell the ranks of an already substantial "floating" population of internal migrant laborers estimated at 100 to 200 million.[31] Those who are lucky to find employment typically live an itinerant existence, many living little better than hand-to-mouth in the construction or service industries. Others are not as fortunate.

As inland incomes stagnate, peasants increasingly are turning to migration to boost their incomes or simply survive. Those from the remotest areas, who have typically not migrated before, are now on the move as well. They are often the most vulnerable, having little experience away from their villages. Some are hoodwinked by unscrupulous private businesses to be their slaves. Unlike the forced labor of China's state-sponsored prison factories, the slave labor in the countryside is little known and reported. It exists mostly in remote areas where underground or semilegal private businesses proliferate.

The earliest reports of slavery surfaced in the mid-1990s. In 1994, as an example, officials of Guangdong province uncovered a vast network of twenty stone quarries where slave labor was the norm. A provincial official interviewed at the time on local radio said that forced labor was "common across the province." In 1996, another quarry in Guangdong was found to have eighty workers in what was described as "a concentration camp." Economist Hu Shudong of the China Economic Research Center at Beijing University said that slavery in China preys on the country's most disadvantaged: "These people are the most honest and sincere, yet they end up getting stuck in the worst possible situation where just living is luck."[32] The growing disaffection of China's workers and peasants is exacerbated by the widening wealth gap and pandemic political corruption. China's poor include 30 million in the rural countryside and a significant number of laid-off workers from the SOEs. Commenting on the growing breach, a *Washington Post* reporter wrote, "A country that once proclaimed itself a workers' paradise has now become a paradise for the well-heeled. After striving to obliterate classes for years, China has become one of the world's most stratified societies with, according to Chinese economists, a gap between rich and poor that dwarfs the divide in the United States." Research by the Chinese Academy of Social Sciences (CASS) in 1991 found that 80 percent of China's $894 billion in bank deposits was held in 20 percent of the accounts. It is reported that in China's major cities many parents indulge their offspring with a monthly allowance of more than $100 per child—the average annual salary for workers. All of which led Zeng Xiangquan, a labor economist at People's University, to warn that "the chasm between rich and poor in this country could have serious political implications."[33]

Corruption is a major factor accounting for the poor circumstances of many disaffected groups. Corruption contributes to the rising incidence of slave labor when slave-users bribe local officials to turn a blind eye; the problem is compounded when the officials themselves have a stake in the operations. As for the SOE workers, many are angered by management's looting of the proceeds from the sale of the assets of inefficient enterprises, instead of distributing them among the workers as required by law. Dai Jianzhong, a CASS sociologist who specializes in labor relations, believes that the culture of corruption is an active factor in the collapse of many SOEs in the first place. As he puts it, "The most important reason for failures is lack of accountability in management, who use power to transfer wealth from workers to themselves."[34]

What particularly galls China's poor and disadvantaged is that they have grounds to suspect that the country's nouveaux riches became so through illegitimate means. A reporter from China's state-run Central Television said that most of the affluent "made their first million by breaking the law." Then there is the close relationship between the moneyed and the Chinese Communist Party. According to one study, many of China's wealthiest are members of the CCP or are relatives or friends of party members and have parlayed their connections into cash.[35] Cases involving the offering of bribes to secure loans from state banks are common. As an example, the former head of the Guangdong provincial branch of China Construction Bank, Dong Huchen, was jailed for thirteen years for accepting $40,000 in bribes to approve loans to private companies totaling $14 million. A particularly egregious case of official corruption was that of a former senior finance official from Yunnan province, Wei Xiaoxiong, who in July 2001 was charged with corruption and abuse of power involving sums totaling almost $150 million. He illegally appropriated $145 million for a company, as well as caused $66.5 million in losses to the state financial fund; he also appointed his mistress to an official post. To cement the collusion of the Communist Party with China's new rich, Jiang Zemin, at a speech commemorating the eightieth anniversary of the CCP in July 2001, proposed that capitalists and entrepreneurs be allowed to become party members. In so doing, Jiang was merely formalizing an arrangement that has been extant for years.[36]

The Persecution of Other Religious Groups

China's marginalized and alienated groups are all ripe for mobilization into new or existing secret societies, including millenarian religious sects. It was Falun Gong's large membership, ability to organize, and facility with modern tools of communication that made it especially alarming to the authorities. But Beijing's suppression of this sect is only the most visible part of a broader effort to control all groups—religious, civil, economic, or social—and to crush any that resists its dominion. Apprehensive about the many problems in society, the leadership can see only its solution in insisting that the people's first loyalty remains with the Communist Party, although few, including even party members, still believe in the official Marxist ideology. Under such conditions, it does not take much to be identified as an outlaw in China. As one commentator wryly observes, all it takes is to advocate democracy, organize an independent labor union, or simply "spend an early-morning hour in a park moving your hands around the shape of an imaginary wheel."[37]

In the early 1990s Beijing began its "antisuperstition" campaign against unregistered religious groups identified as "heretical evil cults" because they had not been approved by the state. Groups that are registered with the government have its authorization and are known as "patriotic" churches or temples. Such groups pay fees to the government, and they must also surrender the names of members as well as have their activities monitored. What information that is available indicates that the number of underground churches far exceeds that of their patriotic counterparts. Religious scholars outside of China believe that the country has 14 million approved Christians (10 million Protestants, 4 million Catholics) and 60 million underground Christians (50 million Protestants, 10 million Catholics). The Chinese government, for its part, claimed a nationwide total of 100 million "religious believers" at the end of 2001.[38]

The antisuperstition campaign has been described by the Chinese people as the most destructive and comprehensive event since controls on religion were relaxed in the late 1970s. Even before the formal banning of Falun Gong and other cults in July 1999, the campaign netted more than 20,000 arrests. In 2001, the annual report by the U.S. Commission on International Religious Freedom confirmed that China's violation of religious freedom had worsened. By the beginning of 2002, according to another account, some 10,000 religious faithful in China had been fined sums ranging from $0.50 to as much as $800,000; 997 believers were placed under surveillance; 4,014 were sentenced to labor reform; 23,686 were arrested (including an eighty-one-year-old Roman Catholic archbishop); more than 20,000 were beaten; 208 became handicapped; and 129 died from the government's abuse.[39]

One of those tortured was Ma Yuqin, a fifty-four-year-old follower of the evangelical Christian South China Church. In an interview with the *New York Times,* she recounted how she was beaten and tormented with electrical shocks. As she was being battered in one room, her son was tortured in the next. Even when she was close to death, she refused to disclose the names of members of her congregation or sign a statement renouncing her faith. Dozens of church members were arrested at the same time and were beaten with clubs, jolted with cattle prods, and burned with cigarettes. Interrogators stomped on the fingers of male prisoners and stripped young women prisoners naked and abused them. A fellow-believer and friend, twenty-seven-year-old Yu Zhongju, died in custody. Ma was released when she became so ill that the authorities feared she would die in prison.[40]

Targets of Beijing's religious suppression go beyond the faithful to include the destruction of buildings and property. In the southeastern coastal region around the city of Wenzhou, it was reported by China's official media that in the course of a month, from November to December 2000, more than 1,500 Christian churches and Buddhist-Daoist temples and shrines were shut down or destroyed. Other religious buildings were seized and converted into schools, recreation centers, or training centers for Communist Party officials. An example was the destruction of a two-story church built in 1982. A crowd of 70 worshipers, many of them weeping, watched behind a line of police officers as workers dismantled their church, tore down its cross, and defaced an inscription from the *Book of Psalms* on the building's facade. In the village of Douxi, another church was forcibly converted into an elementary school when local officials had its wooden cross removed and a red star—the symbol of the Communist Party—painted above the front entrance. One of the congregation's leaders, sixty-two-year-old Hu Songliu, said: "We built this church with our own money, and they just stole it. It's so hard to bear, we all cried."[41]

Among the groups targeted are qigong associations. According to the Hong Kong-based Information Center for Human Rights and Democracy, 185 different qigong groups were "wiped out" in Shaanxi province alone in 2000. Like Falun Gong, most of them combined the practice of breathing exercises with neo-Buddhist and Daoist beliefs. Among them were China Cultivation (Zhong Gong), Nation Cultivation (Guo Gong), Compassion Cultivation (Cibei Gong), Fragrant (Xiang) Gong, Blue Law Society (Falan Hui), and the Goddess of Mercy Law Sect.[42]

Fragrant Gong, based in Luoyang, was reportedly one of the largest qigong sects in China, with more than 10 million members. Its founder, Tian Ruisheng, has been missing since April 2001. Another group, Zhong Gong, briefly became the object of international media attention in the late 1990s when its founder, Zhang Hongbao, fled to Guam and applied for U.S. political asylum. The group began in 1988 and quickly grew into one of the largest legally registered qigong associations in China with more than 1,000 exercise stations, 18,000 teachers, and millions of adherents. Although Zhong Gong attracted many prominent official supporters, including none other than Jiang Zemin who reportedly sought help from a local master in 1992, Beijing began suppressing the group in late 1999, fearing it could become another Falun Gong.[43]

In addition to qigong associations, the campaign also targets more explicitly religious groups. They include the Spirit Church, the Shouters Faction, the Disciples Association, the Holistic Church, Sun Myung Moon's Unification Church, and the White Sun Religion. Even the late Mao Zedong became a figure of popular religious worship, especially in his hometown, Shaoshan, in Hunan province. There, villagers constructed temples to him and included him among the pantheon of kitchen gods and guardian deities of Chinese folk religion. In September 2001, the worshippers of Mao also came under Beijing's attack.[44]

More recently, in 1995, the pogrom was extended to mainstream Christian groups—unregistered Catholic and Protestant "house churches," so named because members meet in each other's homes. They include the China Fangcheng Church (Zhongguo Fangcheng Jiaohui) and the Chinese Evangelical Fellowship (Zhonghua Fuyin Tuanqi). Bishops, priests, and the faithful have been arrested to undergo ideological training and to convince them to become members of government-sanctioned churches. In February 2002, the Vatican's news agency reported that dozens of bishops and priests loyal to Pope John Paul II had been detained, some of them arrested "on no charges, and disappeared ever since." Many more priests were being kept under close police surveillance.[45]

Many of the persecuted groups are messianic, apocalyptic, and millenarian. Among them are the following Christian sects:

- The Shouters Faction (Huhan Pai), also known as Church of God and the Local Assembly. According to confidential Communist Party documents, the Shouters was founded in the United States in 1962 by Li Changshou and was introduced into China in 1979. Four years later, in 1983, the sect had spread to twenty provinces and autonomous regions, with a membership of 200,000. Claiming to be Jesus Christ, Li allegedly encouraged his followers to attack and resist the government; a core member of the sect, Wang Yongmin, allegedly called for "seizing the power from Satan" and the establishment of a new "kingdom." The Shouters gave rise to many splinter groups, including the Established King, Lord God Sect, Power Lord, Oriental Lightning, and the Changshou Sect. In August 2001, thirteen members of the Shouters were detained. Among them were two sect leaders, fifty-five-year-old Wang Xuexiao and fifty-year-old Liu Xishu, who were officially arrested the next month on charges of "using a cult to undermine the enforcement of the law."[46]

▪ The Spirit Church, established in 1983 in Jiangsu province by Hua Xuehe, a farmer and physical education instructor from Henan province. Seven years later, in 1990, the sect had expanded to over thirteen provinces, autonomous regions, and metropolises, including Anhui, Jiangxi, Hunan and Hubei, with a membership totaling 15,000. Hua called himself the second Jesus and claimed to cure illness by exorcizing demons. Members of the church practiced "trembling" and speaking in tongues to summon the Holy Spirit. The group preached that the end of the world would soon arrive and that, in the coming conflagration, God would come to earth to establish "God's nation." In the early 1990s, the authorities cracked down on this sect. Hua and other leaders were imprisoned, charged with "counterrevolutionary hooliganism," "seducing naive women," defrauding property, and "causing people to lose interest in their jobs and livelihoods, thus disrupting social order."[47]

- The Holistic Church, also known as Crying Faction, All Sphere Church, and the Rebirth or Born Again Faction. Founded by Xu Yongze in 1984 in Henan province, the Holistic Church quickly expanded across fifteen provinces, and seven years later had thousands of members. Believers cried aloud as a form of repentance so that they could be born again. Allegedly, Xu called on believers to fight the government, whom he called the enemy, "the devil," and "Red-clothed Monster." This group also believed in the imminent arrival of the end days. Xu was imprisoned or confined to a labor camp many times and was last sentenced in December 1997 to three years' imprisonment for "disturbing social order."[48]

- The New Testament Church, also called Christian Charismatic Evangelistic Band and the Blood and Water of Jesus Christ and Holy Spirit Full Gospel Evangelistic Band. This group was founded in 1960 in Hong Kong by a movie actress, Mei Qi, and a branch was established in mainland China in 1988 by a church leader, Tso Shunkun. In a few years, the sect spread to more than twenty provinces, autonomous regions, and metropolises. The founder and leaders called themselves "prophets" and "rulers of God on the earth." Allegedly, they attacked China's laws as "evil" and the CCP government as a "tyrannical power" and called for its replacement by a "kingdom of God."[49]

- The Established (or Installed) King, a splinter group of the Shouters, founded in 1988 by a former Shouters leader, Wu Yangming. The Established King quickly spread to twenty-nine provinces, autonomous regions, and cities, recruiting believers in the thousands. Wu claimed to be the "Elected King" and that the end of the world was at hand when only believers would be saved and the rest punished and killed. Allegedly, the sect called for the overthrow of the "satanic" Communist Party government and the construction of "a kingdom of God of new heaven and new earth" by the year 2000. The government claimed that Wu raped dozens of adult women and children and defrauded believers of huge sums of money.[50]

- South China Church, a splinter from the Holistic Church, founded in 1988 by Gong Shengliang, a forty-nine-year-old former member of the Holistic Church and native of Hubei province. Calling himself "servant of God, leader, and teacher," Gong advocated the evangelization of China and the Christianization of its culture. Believers were exhorted to "put on the armor given by the Lord" and to "fight a bloody battle with the devil" (the CCP government) and "destroy Satan's kingdom," so as to establish an "everlasting Kingdom of God." According to the Chinese government, this sect was tightly organized into four levels down to the local churches. Allegedly, believers were defrauded of "a huge amount of money," some of it ($39,653) in the form of deposits placed in the sect's private bank, the Bank of Heaven. Sect leaders allegedly raped women and engaged in "other serious criminal activities."[51]

The church, for its part, maintained that authorities confiscated $244,000 (2 million yuan) and seized church properties, arrested more than twenty church leaders, and demolished the homes of five families who gave Gong refuge before he was captured in August 2001. On December 8, 2001, Gong was tried in secret and sentenced to death for rape and "using a cult to sabotage the enforcement of state law." Church members said that the female followers who falsely accused Gong of rape had been tortured with electric batons. Along with Gong, two church organizers (twenty-five-year-old Hu Yong and twenty-six-year-old Xu Fuming) were also condemned to death; thirteen other members received penalties ranging from suspended death sentences to twenty years in prison.[52]

- The Disciples Association (Mentu Hui), founded in 1989 in Shaanxi province by a farmer named Ji Sanbao. Six years later, the sect had expanded to fourteen provinces, with a membership totaling 350,000. Ji allegedly claimed that the end of the world was near and that he was Christ, with the ability to heal the blind and paralyzed and to resurrect the dead. Members believed in rejecting medical treatment in favor of praying. Reportedly, many of the members were detained, assigned to labor camps, or prosecuted. Among them was Xiao Xiuli, a CCP member who, in September 1998, was expelled from the party and dispatched to a labor camp for two years.[53]

- Real God, also called Almighty God, Practical God, and East Lightning. An offshoot from the Shouters, this sect was founded in 1989 by Zhao Weishan, a native of Heilongjiang province. The Real God rapidly expanded to more than ten provinces and cities, with thousands of members. Zhao called himself "powerful Lord" and preached that Jesus had reincarnated as a woman who was the "actual God." Describing China as "a large decadent emperor family dominated by the Big Red Dragon," the sect claimed that the end of the world would come in the year 2000. According to Chinese government documents, the sect was secretly and tightly organized with "suspicious overseas connections." More alarming for the authorities, the sect had made efforts—and succeeded in some areas—to unite with underground Catholic churches.[54]

- Oriental Lightning (Dongfang Shandian), a Christian sect founded in the early 1990s. After its founding, the group rapidly spread across several provinces including Henan, Shaanxi, and Shandong. Members believed that a woman surnamed Deng from Zhengzhou, Henan province, was the Second Coming of Christ, and that her writings were a superior updating of the Bible. The sect reportedly promoted millenarian ideas, with members handing over their savings in anticipation of the end times. Beijing claimed that the sect was "tightly and secretly organized" and that it attacked the government and its religious policy.[55]

- Dami Mission, a Christian group founded in 1988 by a Korean named Lee Jang-lim. In 1992, the group entered China and soon spread to more than ten provinces, autonomous regions, and cities. The sect maintained that the end of the world would arrive at 11 P.M. on October 28, 1992. Believers were organized in "ascending to heaven" groups to await being lifted to heaven with Jesus. Unbelievers would suffer in the coming apocalypse and would be finally judged by Christ in 1999.[56]

- Lord God Sect, another offshoot of the Shouters founded in 1993 by Liu Jiaguo. It rapidly expanded to over twenty-two provinces, autonomous regions, and cities, with a membership in the thousands. Liu claimed to be "God the Lord" and that doomsday was imminent. He allegedly raped nineteen women and defrauded believers. Beijing claimed that the sect was well organized into seven levels.[57]

- Elijah Church (Yiliya Jiao), also known as World Elijah Evangelical Mission. Founded in 1980 by a Korean named Park Myung-ho, this Christian sect arrived in China in 1993 and soon spread to eleven provinces, autonomous regions, and cities, including Liaoning, Jilin, Heilongjiang, Beijing, Hebei, Inner Mongolia, Shandong, Henan, and Shanghai. Park called himself the last prophet "Elijah" and asked believers to worship him as "the Immortal Stone." He called his sect "Stone country," for which he drafted a constitution, national flag, and anthem. Claiming that on September 30, 1997, he would stand up as God, he predicted that the world would end in 2000. Reportedly, he vowed to "dash and ruin every nation," including China and its government. The sect, according to Beijing, was well financed and well organized into eight communal villages comprised of hundreds of believers in northeastern China.[58]

- Three Kinds of Servants Sect, founded by Xu Wenku, a native of Henan province. The sect spread to eighteen provinces, autonomous regions, and cities. Reportedly Xu deified himself by calling himself "chief servant" of God. He preached that the world would end with seven disasters by 2000, and Jesus would lift only believers to heaven, leaving unbelievers to "go down to hell." The sect allegedly defrauded believers and committed other unspecified crimes of "disturbing public order."

In addition to these Christian groups, there are apocalyptic groups that are Buddhist-Daoist, including the following:

- The Immortal Real Buddha Sect, founded in 1979 in the United States in Seattle by a Chinese-American named Lu Shengyan. This sect entered China in 1988 and quickly spread to more than thirteen provinces and cities. Proclaiming himself "Buddha incarnate," Lu allegedly publicly attacked the CCP government in many speeches in 1989.[59]

- Goddess of Mercy Law Sect (Guanyin Famen), founded in Taiwan in 1988 by Shi Qinghai, a Chinese woman of British nationality. This Buddhist sect rapidly expanded to most of mainland China's provinces, autonomous regions and metropolises. In 1998, one of its core members, Xu Chengjiang, created a branch that extended to nine provinces and cities. Both Shi and Xu claimed to be living gods. Shi was the "Supreme Teacher," equal in status to Buddha Sakyamuni, Jesus, and Allah. For her part, Xu also claimed to be "a contemporary living Buddha." The two leaders allegedly called for the overthrow of the Communist Party government, which they compared to the devil. Claiming that doomsday was impending and that only those who joined the sect would be saved, they urged believers to sell their houses and live in mountains with their families to escape the impending apocalypse.[60]

There are also qigong associations and other apocalyptic groups not identifiable with any established religions. They include:

- Compassion Gong, founded in 1997 by Xiao Yun in Hubei province. This qigong group expanded to Hunan and Jiangxi provinces, attracting 900 members. Its teachings were reportedly copied from Falun Gong and included the latter's doomsday ideas. In September 1999, Xiao was arrested as a rapist for allegedly deceiving four women into having sex with him.[61]

- Shenchang Human Body Science Group, a qigong group with 5 million members, described as an evil cult by the government. Its leader, Shen Chang, was arrested in July 2000 in Suzhou on suspicion of tax evasion. When authorities found out he headed a qigong group, they added an additional charge of "using an evil cult to destroy legal procedures." On September 18, 2001, Shen was convicted and sentenced to twelve years in prison.[62]

- The Children of God (also known as The Family of Love), founded in the United States in 1968 by an American, David Moses Berg. The group entered China in 1980. Berg claimed that he received a revelation from God to deify himself as the "emperor." According to the Chinese government, Berg "vilified communism" and urged believers to use sex to recruit others into his family. He also preached that doomsday was at hand and that believers should cast off everything and offer their bodies and property in absolute obedience to his "imperial family."[63]

A Self-Fulfilling Policy?

The proliferation of apocalyptic millenarian groups in China with membership in the thousands and millions further confirms the prevalence of deep-seated ills in Chinese society and of the Chinese people's hunger for spiritual solace. One can only imagine the depths of despair that could convince millions that the end of the world is imminent. An indicator of that despair is the country's high suicide rate. In October 2001, PRC Vice Minister of Health Yin Dakui reported that China had one of the highest rates in the world, at 1 per 100,000. Each year, at least 2 million failed in suicide attempts, while a quarter of a million succeeded. Sadly, the rates were higher among women, especially in rural areas, and among the elderly and the young. Those figures, according to Yin, reflected a growing tide of depression, anxiety, and feelings of failure.[64]

The stubborn appeal of religion in an officially atheistic country also speaks to the need of human beings to believe in something larger than themselves and that their lives have transcendental meaning and purpose. That is something the Communist Party cannot provide. There was a time when the people held the party and its Marxist creed in religious reverence. But they have paid dearly for their devotion. More than that, to many, the party has abandoned its convictions: it now worships a new idol, Mammon. Having become empty materialists, the Communist Party leaders find threatening any and all who aspire to a purpose higher and nobler than Deng Xiaping's injunction that "to get rich is glorious." As one scholar put it: "The bottom line . . . is that the Chinese government is very fragile, in spite of all their claims to be powerful. China may be a police state, but it is a fragile one. The Communists feel that . . . the people are really tired of them. [The party has] deprived the people of every other spiritual outlet [and] no longer has an audience that believes in the Communist myth."[65]

Falun Gong and other faith-based groups are clearly filling a spiritual need that Communist ideology no longer satisfies. A Falun Gong practitioner, Sophie Xiao, gave expression to that need when she described her experiences to a reporter. Her life had been tragic, though typical of many Chinese of her generation. During the Cultural Revolution—her formative years—her father went mad after he was denounced at work as being disloyal to Mao. He regularly took his frustrations out by beating his daughter and his wife. Xiao became self-destructive, but she eventually found serenity in Falun Gong. Her new-found faith, she said, gave her "answers to things I had been looking for all my life. . . . It changes you. You let go of a lot of human desires and become very peaceful, and then you don't fear anything. That's probably what the Chinese government is afraid of."[66]

China's leaders give every indication of having a keen sense of history. No doubt they are mindful that in the country's past, millenarian sects and other religious groups had overturned dynasties, beginning with the first sectarian revolt by the Yellow Turbans in A.D. 184 to the more recent Taiping and Boxer rebellions in the twentieth century. No doubt the Communist Party fears a repetition.

Yet if anything is likely to bring about rebellion, it is the government's actions in response to the people's irrepressible quest for numinous meaning. In persecuting Falun Gong and other religious groups, the Chinese Communist Party has demonstrated that it is just as intolerant of "heterodox" faiths as the emperors of Imperial China. And just as its Imperial predecessors discovered, by suppressing religious groups that refuse to submit to its control, the

Communist Party government today also risks creating the very outcome it fears. It is politicizing groups that hitherto had been solely occupied with the supernatural and, in so doing, driving them underground and transforming them into determined opponents. As an academic in Beijing rues, "The government is turning [Falun Gong] into an anticommunist cause. . . . It's a stupid policy. It is creating enemies where there were no enemies."[67]

Falun Gong's founder, Li Hongzhi, concurs with that observation, noting that the government, by treating ordinary citizens as its enemy, is "raising the stakes" and pushing millions to "the opposing side." At the same time as he expresses hope that his disciples refrain from confronting the state, he insists that they continue their peaceful protests. According to Li, "if the Chinese government continues like this and begins to kill people," it would be difficult for him to predict the consequences. "There could be another Tiananmen incident . . . [and] the masses will lose their confidence in the government."[68]

Commenting on the Falun Gong phenomenon and evidently knowledgeable about the role that millenarian movements had played in Chinese history, a writer for the *Economist* offered the following prediction: "It may yet turn out that the seeds of Chinese communism's eventual collapse will have been sown, not by market economists or human-rights activists in the West, but by weird millenarians, inspired by Chinese traditions, in China itself."[69]

The problem is that if the Communist Party is overthrown, it will probably not be by a democratic group. This is because Beijing's suppression of civil society has forced autonomous groups to go underground—and groups that must operate in secrecy cannot be democratically organized if they are to survive against a hostile, determined, and powerful opponent.

Falun Gong is an example of the kind of outlawed but undemocratic groups that can survive in contemporary China. Although there can no justification for the Chinese government's brutal treatment of this sect, this does not mean that the sect itself is a paragon of virtue. Despite its professed commitment to tolerance and forbearance, Falun Gong has displayed a disturbing penchant for bullying its critics and for vindictiveness. The case of Sima Nan, a champion of the 1989 democracy movement, is an example. He took upon himself the task of exposing religious frauds by offering a handsome reward to anyone, including those in Falun Gong, who could produce a genuine paranormal effect that he could not duplicate or expose. For that, he was viciously denounced by Falun Gong and cursed by its founder. For all his avowed godliness, Li Hongzhi wished, under the guise of a prediction, that Sima would be stricken with lameness and blindness. Li also claimed to have secretly inserted a wheel, revolving in the wrong direction, in Sima's abdomen.[70]

The necessarily undemocratic nature of viable opposition movements might account for Chinese history's peculiar and persistent cyclical quality long noted by sinologists. Throughout the thousands of years of its history, periods of unity would alternate with episodes of fragmentation.[71] Dynasties were born, flourished, and decayed, each giving way to a successor in a convulsion of populist insurrection. The peasant rebellions that overthrew dynasties were oddly lacking in ideology or class consciousness—the rebels opposed the ruling dynasty but not the system of government, convinced that it was the reigning emperor's vices that had led Heaven to withdraw its mandate. In effect, the rebels understood the problem as one of personality instead of being systemic. Given that understanding, they were convinced that what was needed was not the instauration of a new form of government, but the replacement of a morally bankrupt dynasty with another founded by a man of virtue, the leader of the rebellion.

The denouement of every dynasty was marked by a series of increasingly intractable crises and disasters. These included a precipitous decline in the availability of revenue, disintegration of the hydraulic system, and a corresponding failure of agricultural production. All of this would be attended by an increase in banditry that took on more and more organized forms until active resistance threatened the very continuity of the dynasty. The mass migration of peasants, no longer able to sustain themselves through their traditional pursuits, brought recruits to peasant armies. Communication from the provinces to the center could no longer be sustained; more and more local revenue failed to reach the capital. Corruption increased and further undermined the effectiveness of government, which was no longer capable of ensuring order and of responding to even relatively minor natural dislocations and disasters. Giving expression and organization to the popular disaffection were secret societies and millenarian movements. It was said that Heaven had withdrawn its mandate to rule.

China today is a country rife with contradictions. In the midst of economic prosperity—a boom that remains largely confined to the coastal cities—many still labor under heartbreaking hardships and deprivation. More troubling, the country seems to be displaying some of the same signs of blight that historically marked the end of dynasties. The decay notwithstanding, it would be foolhardy to predict that the end of Communist Party rule is imminent.

Nevertheless, as long as the societal problems that engender the rise of millenarian sects persist—and the Chinese government continues its suppression of civil society, including the persecution of religions—the likelihood is that even if Beijing succeeds at fully eradicating Falun Gong, similar religious movements undoubtedly will arise in the future. As Li Hongzhi said, "They can lock people up . . . but they can't lock up their hearts."[72] By continuing the traditional Chinese state's intolerance of "heterodox" faiths, the Communist Party may well come to reap the same fate. It may discover that, by politicizing and driving underground unapproved religious and other groups, it is hastening the time when such groups, like the roiling flood waters of the Yellow River, eventually break through the dikes to directly challenge the state.

NOTES

Chapter One
A Religious Sect Defies the State

1. The demonstrators came mainly from northern China—from Beijing, Tianjin and other parts of Hobei, Honan, Shandong, and Shanxi. Gong Yue, "Falun Gong shijian dizhen yu sisuo" (The Shocking and Thought-Provoking Falun Gong Incident), *Beijing zhichun (Beijing Spring)*, no. 73, June 1999, p. 32. Falun Gong publications include *Zhuan Falun (Rotating the Law Wheel)*, *Zhongguo Falun Gong (China Falun Gong)*, *Falun Dafa (Falun Great Law)*, *Falun Fofa (Falun Buddha Law)*, and *Dayuan Manfa (Great Circle Complete Law)*. The last two books are Falun Gong's textbooks.

2. Isabel Hilton, "The Sect That Scares China's Leaders," *New Statesman* 128, September 6, 1999, p. 16.

3. Leslie Pappas, "The Power of the 'Force,'" *Newsweek International*, May 10, 1999, p. 42. In the United States, the Chinese immigrant community make up the majority of Falun Gong followers, although Americans from non-Chinese backgrounds have joined the movement in steadily increasing numbers. Precise numbers are hard to come by because Falun Gong does not keep membership rolls. Practice groups have a presence in American cities as diverse as New York; Louisville, Ky.; Cleveland; Orlando, Fla.; Salt Lake City; and Portland, Ore. Nanaho Sawano, "Tracing Falun Gong's Roots in the U.S.," *Christian Science Monitor* (hereafter *CSM*), January 6, 2000, p. 18.

4. "They Cannot Lock Up Hearts," *Newsweek International,* August 2, 1999, p. 42. Jay Nordlinger, "Crackdown Time: Why Beijing Fears the Falun Gong," *National Review,* September 27, 1999, p. 24.

5. Nordlinger, "Crackdown Time," 24.

6. Daniel Reid, *A Complete Guide to Chi-Gung* (Boston: Shambhala, 2000), 5.

7. Pappas, "Power of the 'Force,' " 42. Bay Fang, "An Opiate of the Masses?" *U.S. News and World Report* (hereafter *USNWR*), February 22, 1999, p. 45.

8. Gordon White, "The Dynamics of Civil Society in Post-Mao China," in Brian Hook, ed., *The Individual and the State in China* (Oxford: Clarendon Press, 1996), 206. John Leicester, " 'Green' Movement Arising in China," *San Francisco Examiner,* November 29, 1998, p. A22.

9. Fang, "Opiate of the Masses?" 45.

10. *San Francisco Chronicle* (hereafter *SFC*), January 20, 2000, p. A16; "Chinese Sect Members Appeal to Bush over Detained Leader," *Inside China Today* (hereafter *ICT*), February 2, 2001. *ICT* is a Web-based service that provides subscribers with news reports from such agencies as Agence France Presse and Reuters.

11. Gayle M. B. Hanson, "China Shaken by Mass Meditation," *Insight on the News,* August 23, 1999, p. 24.

12. Ibid.

13. Ibid.

14. Fang, "Opiate of the Masses?" 45.

15. "A Chinese Taste of That New-Time Religion," *USNWR,* February 22, 1999, p. 46.

16. Hanson, "China Shaken by Mass Meditation"; "China Bans Publications on Falun Gong," *Xinhua News Agency,* July 23, 1999.

17. David Van Biema and Jaime A. FlorCruz, "The Man with the Qi," *Time,* May 10, 1999, p. 74.

18. "China Bans Publications on Falun Gong."

19. Pappas, "Power of the 'Force,' " 42.

20. Van Biema and FlorCruz, "Man with the Qi," 74.

21. Terry McCarthy and Mia Turner, "Inside the Falun Gong," *Time,* August 9, 1999, p. 48. Nordlinger, "Crackdown Time," 24.

22. Charles Hutzler, "Beijing's Assaults Appear Successful in Breaking Down Spiritual Group," *Wall Street Journal* (hereafter *WSJ*), April 26, 2001. Ian Johnson, "How One Chinese City Resorted to Atrocities to Control Falun Dafa," *WSJ,* December 26, 2000.

23. "China Cracks Down on Falun Gong Sect," *Christian Century,* July 28, 1999, p. 740; Hanson, "China Shaken by Mass Meditation."

24. Hanson, "China Shaken by Mass Meditation"; Bay Fang, "Spooked by a Curious Cult," *USNWR,* August 2, 1999, p. 42.

25. "China's Crackdown on Falun Gong Takes On Draconian Proportions," *ICT,* February 13, 2001. McCarthy and Turner, "Inside the Falun Gong," 48; Hanson, "China Shaken by Mass Meditation"; "China Sets Reward for Arrest of Sect Leader," *Christian Century,* August 11, 1999, p. 771; Melinda Liu, Jeffrey Bartholet, and Leslie Pappas, "Mao versus the Mystic," *Newsweek,* August 9, 1999, p. 43.

26. "China's Trial of Faith," *Economist,* November 6, 1999, p. 41; "China Issues Anti-Cult Law to Combat Falun Gong and Other Movements Regime Deems Undesirable," *International Law Update* 5:12, December 1999.

27. Hanson, "China Shaken by Mass Meditation." McCarthy and Turner, "Inside the Falun Gong," 48. Liu, Bartholet, and Pappas, "Mao versus the Mystic," 43.

28. McCarthy and Turner, "Inside the Falun Gong," 48; Fang, "Spooked by a Curious Cult," 42. "Chinese Government Continues Persecution of the Falun Gong Sect," *Lancet,* February 26, 2000, p. 733.

29. "China Issues Anti-Cult Law to Combat Falun Gong and Other Movements Regime Deems Undesirable," *International Law Update,* 5:12, December 1999. "China's Trial of Faith"; Charles Hutzler, "Organizers of Sect Sentenced in China," *SFC,* December 27, 1999, p. A1.

30. Charles Hutzler, "Falun Gong Accuses Police of Torture," *SFC,* October 29, 1999, pp. A1, A7; "China Uses New Law against Falun Gong," *SFC,* November 1, 1999, p. A11. "China Uses 'Rule of Law' to Justify Falun Gong Crackdown," *Human Rights Watch,* November 9, 1999.

31. "China Uses 'Rule of Law.'"

32. "China Jails Judge for Seven Years over Falun Gong Books," *ICT,* February 6, 2001.

33. "China: Gong, but Not Forgotten," *Economist* (U.S.), April 29, 2000, p. 39.

34. Christopher Hitchens, "For Whom the Gong Tolls," *Nation,* November 20, 2000, p. 9. "China: Gong, but Not Forgotten," 39. "Falun Gong Members Arrested for Protesting," *SFC,* December 11, 2000, p. A14. "China Police Arrest Falun Demonstrators," *Washington Times,* January 1, 2001.

35. Craig S. Smith, "Sect Clings to the Web in the Face of Beijing's Ban," *New*

York Times (hereafter *NYT*), July 5, 2001. Craig S. Smith, "Beijing Protest by Falun Sect Brings Arrest of Hundreds," *NYT,* October 2, 2000.

36. Craig S. Smith, "Banned Chinese Sect Is Spurred On by Exiled Leader," *NYT,* January 5, 2001; Mahlon Meyer, Russell Watson, and Kevin Platt, "China Wakes Up a Tiger," *Newsweek,* February 5, 2001, p. 33.

37. Robert Marquand, "China's Image-Polishing Collides with Protests," *CSM,* January 24, 2001, p. 1.

38. "China Jails 37 Who Spread Falun Gong Fliers," *ICT,* March 2, 2001.

39. "Falun Gong Members' Fiery Revolt in Tiananmen," *SFC,* January 24, 2001, p. A1. "China Accuses Falun Gong of Provoking Violence," *SFC,* December 6, 2001, p. A7; Craig S. Smith, "China Attacks Falun Gong in New Public Relations Effort," *NYT,* January 11, 2001.

40. Charles Hutzler, "China Moves to Keep Falun Gong in Check," *SFC,* January 25, 2001, p. A12. "Falun Gong Member Sets Himself Ablaze," *SFC,* February 17, 2001, p. A13.

41. Peter Wonacott, "China's Government Reveals Detailed Report of Burn Protest," *WSJ,* January 31, 2001.

42. Smith, "Banned Chinese Sect Is Spurred On by Exiled Leader."

43. Fifty-seven-year-old Liu Yunfang received a life sentence, fifty-year-old Wang Jindong was sentenced to fifteen years in prison, forty-nine-year-old Xue Hongjun to ten years, and thirty-four-year-old Liu Xiuqin to seven years. A fifth defendant, Liu Baorong, received no penalty because she had confessed and "exposed other criminals involved in the case," the court said. Erik Eckholm, "China Court Finds Four in Falun Gong Guilty of Murder," *SFC,* August 18, 2001, p. A10.

44. On March 18, 2001, two months after her self-immolation, it was reported that the girl died of "heart troubles" from sustaining burns on 40 percent of her body and severe damage to her windpipe. "Girl Who Immolated Herself in Beijing Dies," *NYT,* March 19, 2001.

45. "Beijing Recruits Youth to Fight Falun Gong," *ICT,* February 18, 2001. "China Mobilizes Masses to Denounce Falun Gong," *ICT,* February 1, 2001. "China Rewards 1,600 Anti-Falun Gong Fighters," *ICT,* February 26, 2001. "China Hosts UN Rights Chief, Vows to Wipe Out Sect," *ICT,* February 27, 2001. "China's Crackdown on Falun Gong Takes On Draconian Proportions," *ICT,* February 13, 2001.

46. Erik Eckholm, "Foreign Media Role Cited in Beijing Immolation," *NYT,* February 9, 2001. Gren Manuel, "Dutch Delegation Cancels China Trip after

Beijing Attacks Falun Dafa Visit," *WSJ*, February 7, 2001. Erik Eckholm, "China Steps Up War on Sect, but Some Denounce Attacks," *NYT*, February 7, 2001. "Grip Tightens on Media," *Far Eastern Economic Review* (hereafter *FEER*), February 28, 2002.

47. "China Jails 37 Who Spread Falun Gong Fliers," *ICT*, March 2, 2001. On March 9, 2001, Falun Gong's office in New York categorically denied that the sect was funded by the U.S. government. In a statement to Reuters, the sect insisted, "No evidence for this blatant fabrication was offered, because none exists." "Falun Gong Denies U.S. Congress Gave It Funding," *NYT*, March 9, 2001.

48. "China Says Taiwan Vice President Colluding with Falun Gong," *ICT*, March 26, 2001.

49. "China Steps Up Falun Gong Crackdown with New Guidelines," *ICT*, June 11, 2001.

50. "Directive Targets Falun Gong Cult," *China Daily*, June 11, 2001. "Falun Gong Follower Sentenced to Death," *SFC*, August 23, 2001, p. A9.

51. "Some 130 Falun Gong on Hunger Strike at Chinese Camp," *ICT*, August 10, 2001. "Chinese Cops Beat Backers of Falun Gong," *SFC*, April 26, 2001, p. A14.

52. "Falun Gong Follower Sets Self on Fire, Dies," *WSJ*, July 23, 2001.

53. "China Jails 37 Who Spread Falun Gong Fliers," *ICT*, March 2, 2001; "China Arrests 6 Falun Gong Followers," *NYT*, March 9, 2001.

54. Philip P. Pan, "Falun Gong Members Receive Stiff Sentences," *Washington Post*, September 20, 2002; Christopher Bodeen, "Arrests in Falun Gong TV Incident," *SFC*, April 3, 2002, p. A9; "Falun Gong Activists Break into TV System," *SFC*, May 11, 2002, p. A16.

55. "Falun Gong Leader Calls China Crackdown Futile," *ICT*, March 7, 2001; "China Jails 13 More Falun Gong Activists," *ICT*, March 13, 2001. "Falun Gong Leader Savages 'Wicked' Chinese Leadership," *ICT*, March 15, 2001.

56. "Falun Gong Slams China for 'Evil Persecution,' " *NYT*, January 14, 2001.

57. The text of the BBC report entitled, "CPPCC Standing Committee Member Xu Simin Says Falun Gong Is a Political Organization," published on the Web site of the Hong Kong newspaper *Ta Kung Pao* on February 1, 2001. "Falun Gong Activities in Hong Kong Aimed at Central Government, Beijing Claims," *ICT*, February 6, 2001. "For Whom the Gong Tolls," *Economist*, February 17, 2001, p. 46.

58. "Hong Kong Government Will Watch Falun Gong Movement Very Closely," *WSJ*, February 8, 2001.

59. "Hong Kong Prepares Law to Ban Falun Gong," *ICT*, April 27, 2001. "Hong Kong Leader Says Falun Gong a Cult, No Plans to Ban," *ICT*, June 14, 2001.

60. Hutzler, "Beijing's Assaults Appear Successful in Breaking Down Spiritual Group"; "China Locking Up Falun Gong Members in Mental Hospitals," *ICT*, February 19, 2001.

61. "They Cannot Lock Up Hearts," *Newsweek International*, August 2, 1999, p. 42. Johnson, "How One Chinese City Resorted to Atrocities."

62. Bodeen, "Arrests in Falun Gong TV Incident"; "Falun Gong Member Dies in Chinese Police Custody," *ICT*, August 3, 2001; "Falun Gong Claims Eight More Deaths in Chinese Police Custody," *ICT*, November 28, 2001.

63. Christopher Bodeen, "Hundreds Mourn Falun Gong Member," *SFC*, December 14, 2000, p. C8.

64. "Falun Gong Member Dies in Police Detention in Northeast China," *ICT*, June 15, 2001.

65. Johnson, "How One Chinese City Resorted to Atrocities"; "Reports of Deaths of Falun Gong Detainees," *San Francisco Examiner*, July 27, 2000; "China Frees Canadian Sect Follower; Group Says Three More Died in Custody," *WSJ*, January 11, 2001; "Seven More Falun Gong Followers Die in Chinese Custody," *ICT*, February 7, 2001; "Falun Gong Member Dies in Chinese Police Custody," *ICT*, August 3, 2001; "Two Falun Gong Members Die during Detention," *SFC*, September 1, 2001 "Six Falun Gong Followers Die in Police Custody," *ICT*, September 19, 200; "Detained Falun Gong Follower Dies after Suspected Force-Feeding," *ICT*, September 28, 2001; "Falun Gong Follower Thrown to Death by Police," *ICT*, October 1, 2001.

66. Craig S. Smith, "Falun Gong Deaths Set Off Dispute on Suicide Reports," *NYT*, July 4, 2001. "China Says Three Falun Gong Died in Mass Suicide Attempt," *ICT*, July 5, 2001.

67. Johnson, "How One Chinese City Resorted to Atrocities."

68. "Falun Gong Denounces Torture and Abuse of Its Female Followers," *ICT*, April 10, 2001.

69. "China Vows 'War to the End' with Falun Gong," *ICT*, February 12, 2001. "Falun Gong Followers Seek Refuge in Private from China's Crackdown," *ICT*, February 7, 2001.

70. Richard Madsen observed that it is Falun Gong's "decentralized network of local groups, linked through cadres of leaders at different levels of the network" that makes it a "tremendously supple organization." Interestingly, Madsen also noted that this kind of loose organization had been used by

Chinese peasant rebels in times past and by the CCP in the 1920s and 1930s. See Richard Madsen, "Demystifying Falun Gong," *Current History,* September 2000, p. 246.

71. Smith, "Sect Clings to the Web in the Face of Beijing's Ban." David Murphy, "Losing Battle," *FEER,* February 15, 2001. Frank Ching, "Falun Gong: Giant vs. Ghost," *FEER,* February 22, 2001.

72. Murphy, "Losing Battle."

Chapter Two
Chinese Religions and Millenarian Movements

1. C. K. Yang, "The Functional Relationship between Confucian Thought and Chinese Religion," in John K. Fairbank, ed., *Chinese Thought and Institutions* (Chicago: University of Chicago Press, 1967), 270.

2. Ibid., 276, 270.

3. Ibid., 272–73.

4. Anne Birrel, *Chinese Mythology: An Introduction* (Baltimore: Johns Hopkins University Press, 1993), 32, 25, 23–24; and Anthony Christie, "China," in Richard Cavendish, ed., *Mythology: An Illustrated Encyclopedia* (New York: Barnes and Noble, 1993), 37, 40.

5. C. K. Yang, *Religion in Chinese Society* (Berkeley: University of California Press, 1967), 106.

6. J. J. M. De Groot, *The Religious System of China* (Taipei: Southern Materials Center, 1989), 3, 30, 28, 40.

7. Ibid., 3–5.

8. Ibid., 272–73.

9. Ibid., 325, 327–30.

10. Marcel Granet, *The Religion of the Chinese People* (New York: Harper and Row, 1975), 120. De Groot, *Religious System of China,* 9.

11. Granet, *Religion of the Chinese People,* 101–2.

12. Ibid., 103.

13. Ibid., 109, 108.

14. Ibid., 114, 115.

15. Ibid., 97.

16. Jean Chesneaux, *Peasant Revolts in China 1840–1949* (New York: W. W. Norton, 1973), 9. James F. Rinehart, *Revolution and the Millennium: China, Mexico, and Iran* (Westport, Conn.: Praeger, 1997), 68.

17. Granet, *Religion of the Chinese People,* 101–4, 109, 117, 34.

18. Ibid., 120, 130, 122, 125–26.

19. Ibid., 34–35, 128–30.

20. Ibid., 124–26.

21. Ibid., 120–21, 127–28.

22. Ibid., 35, 132–33.

23. Ibid., 133–34, 136.

24. Ibid., 136–37.

25. Ibid., 142, 141.

26. Ibid., 142–43.

27. It is for that reason that Karl Wittfogel called the absolutist government in Imperial China an example of "oriental despotism." See Karl A. Wittfogel, *Oriental Despotism* (New Haven: Yale University Press, 1967).

28. David Ownby, *Brotherhoods and Secret Societies in Early and Mid-Qing China: The Formation of a Tradition* (Stanford: Stanford University Press, 1996), 2.

29. Restrictions and controlling measures imposed on religions include: the issuance of edicts and outright suppression; the licensing of all ordained priests; the surrendering of a priest's ordination certificate to the government upon his death; state supervision of priestly activities and conduct; the restriction of Buddhist and Daoist priests to one neophyte per priest (which ensured that the priesthood would be kept at the self-replacing level at best); government approval for the construction of temples, even those with private funds; social and political discrimination against priests, magicians, sorcerers, and seers. Yang, *Religion in Chinese Society,* 187–92.

30. "China's Trial of Faith," *Economist,* November 6, 1999, p. 41.

31. During the reign of Mao Zedong, however, governmental power penetrated down to the lowest (village) level. After his death, the great communes were dismantled, and the reach of the state reverted back to China's millenial tradition, stopping at the county level.

32. In Imperial China, the state had regulations governing many aspects of daily life: dress, the colors of clothing, the dimensions of public and private buildings, festivals, music, birth, and death. Etienne Balazs, *Chinese Civilization and Bureaucracy* (New Haven: Yale University Press, 1964), 10–11. In spite of the freer lives of the people in the PRC today, when it chooses to, the government still interferes in private affairs. A recent example is the passage, in April 2001, by China's legislature of sweeping changes to the Marriage

Law. Those changes make extramarital affairs illegal by prohibiting married Chinese from living with someone other than their spouse. "China Passes Reforms to Curb Rampant Extramarital Affairs," *Inside China Today*, April 28, 2001.

33. For a definition of "ideocracy," see Jaroslaw Piekalkiewicz and Alfred Wayne Penn, *Politics of Ideocracy* (Albany: State University of New York, 1995), 27.

34. For a detailed account of China's turn to patriotic nationalism, see chapters 1, 8, 9, and 10 of Maria Hsia Chang, *Return of the Dragon: China's Wounded Nationalism* (Boulder: Westview Press, 2001).

35. It should be noted that *yiduan*, the Chinese expression for heterodoxy, literally means "heresy." In effect, all non-Confucian religions were regarded as "heretical" cults. More than being heretical, the heterodox faiths were regarded as evil cults because *xiejiao*, the Chinese expression for "cult," includes the attribute of evil (*xie*).

36. Ownby, *Brotherhoods and Secret Societies*, 2. Rinehart, *Revolution and the Millennium*, 69.

37. Jean Chesneaux, ed., *Popular Movements and Secret Societies in China, 1840–1950* (Stanford: Stanford University Press, 1972). Rinehart, *Revolution and the Millennium*, 70.

38. Ownby, *Brotherhoods and Secret Societies*, 4; Chesneaux, *Peasant Revolts in China*, 18.

39. Ownby, *Brotherhoods and Secret Societies*, 2–3. Rinehart, *Revolution and the Millennium*, 19, 22.

40. Ibid., 31; Anthony F. C. Wallace, "Revitalization Movements," *American Anthropologist* 58 (1956), p. 626.

41. Rinehart, *Revolution and the Millennium*, 32–33.

42. See Robert Jay Lifton, "Death and History," in Ernest A. Menze, ed., *Totalitarianism Reconsidered* (Port Washington, N.Y.: Kennikat, 1981), 206–30.

43. Rinehart, *Revolution and the Millennium*, 69–70.

44. Ibid., 68–69, 70.

45. Susan Naquin, *Millenarian Rebellion in China: The Eight Trigrams Uprising of 1813* (New Haven: Yale University Press, 1976), 2, 8.

46. Susan Naquin maintained that the mother goddess was also known as Xiwangmu (Mother Ruler of the West) and Wangmu niangniang (Empress Mother Ruler). Other authors, however, insist that Xiwangmu and Wangmu niangniang referred to an entirely separate goddess unrelated to the Eternal Mother of the White Lotus. See Zong Jin, Wang Yu, and Li Qian, eds.,

Huaxia nuxian (*Chinese Goddesses*) (Taiyuan: Beiyue wenyi, 1994), 31–34, 109–14.

47. Naquin, *Millenarian Rebellion in China*, 9–10.

48. Ibid., 10.

49. Ibid., 11–13. It is interesting that there is an European counterpart to the White Lotus belief in three successive stages of human history. In the late twelfth century, a Calabrian abbot and hermit, Joachim of Fiore, provided an important doctrinal foundation for Western millenarianism. The Joachiate prophecy stated that history involved three successive stages, each of them presided over by one of the Persons of the Holy Trinity. The first was the Age of the Father or of the law, an age of excessive fear and bondage for all people. The second was the Age of the Son or of the Gospel, one of faith and final submission. The third era, which was yet to come, would be the Age of the (Holy) Spirit, one of love, joy, and freedom, "when the knowledge of God would be revealed directly in the hearts of all men." In effect, the third era would be the much-anticipated millennium that immediately follows Christ's Second Coming. Rinehart, *Revolution and the Millennium*, 22.

50. Li was the surname of the ruling family of the Tang dynasty, as well as the traditional surname of Laozi, the founder of Daoism. Laozi was a messianic figure to some popular religious sects, believed by them to be a god who would be reborn on earth to save humanity. Naquin, *Millenarian Rebellion in China*, 15, 2. It is in this context that the family name of Falun Gong's founder, Li Hongzhi, takes on significance.

51. Barbara E. Ward, "Chinese Secret Societies," in Norman MacKenzie, ed., *Secret Societies* (London: Aldus Books, 1967), 216, 224; Rinehart, *Revolution and the Millennium*, 70.

52. Ownby, *Brotherhoods and Secret Societies*, 3. John Robert Shepherd, *Statecraft and Political Economy on the Taiwan Frontier* (Stanford: Stanford University Press, 1993), 4.

53. Naquin, *Millenarian Rebellion in China*, 12–13.

54. Ibid., 1, 7, 2.

55. For a more detailed account of the Opium War and its initiation of China's Hundred Years of Humiliation (by Western and Japanese imperialism), see chapter 4 of Chang, *Return of the Dragon*. Guenther Lewy, *Religion and Revolution* (New York: Oxford University Press, 1974), 155. Rinehart, *Revolution and the Millennium*, 71.

56. *The Revolution of 1911* (Beijing: Foreign Languages Press, 1976), 2–3.

57. V. G. Kiernan, *The Lords of Human Kind: Black Man, Yellow Man and White Man in an Age of Empire* (Boston: Little, Brown, 1969), 162. Ssu-yu Teng and John K. Fairbank, *China's Response to the West: A Documentary Survey 1839–1923* (New York: Atheneum, 1973), 65–66.

58. Chesneaux, *Peasant Revolts in China*, 52.

59. *Revolution of 1911*, 4.

60. Rinehart, *Revolution and the Millennium*, 80; Fei-ling Davis, *Primitive Revolutionaries of China* (Honolulu: University Press of Hawaii, 1977), 178, 171.

61. Rinehart, *Revolution and the Millennium*, 69–70.

62. "Protests in Tiananmen Square," *Economist*, January 27, 2001, p. 43.

63. Barend ter Haar, professor of Chinese history at Leiden University, has a dissenting view on Falun Gong's millenarianism. He maintains that because the sect does not specify a date for the end time, it does not qualify as truly millenarian. (See his Web site on Falun Gong: www.let/leidenuniv.nl/bth/ falun.htm.) The problem is that the professor's definition for "millenarian" is not shared by the scholars cited in this chapter who have written on millenarian movements.

Chapter Three
Falun Gong: Beliefs and Practices

1. Leslie Pappas, "The Power of the 'Force,'" *Newsweek International*, May 10, 1999, p. 42.

2. *Falun Dafa Yijie* (*The Meaning and Explanation of Great Law of the Wheel*) (Hong Kong: Falun Fofa, 1997), 104.

3. *Falun Dafa Yijie*, 104. Li Hongzhi, *Zhuan Falun Fajie* (*Explaining Rotating the Law Wheel*) (Hong Kong: Falun Fofa, 1997), 165.

4. Li, *Zhuan Falun Fajie*, 201.

5. Li Hongzhi, *Falun Buddha Law* (Hong Kong: Falun Fo Fa, 1999), 50.

6. Ibid., 20–21.

7. Ibid., 50–51; Li Hongzhi, *Falun Fofa* (*Falun Buddha Law*) (Hong Kong: Falun Fofa, 1999), 4–5.

8. Li, *Falun Buddha Law*, 49, 51; *Zhuan Falun Fajie*, 29.

9. Li Hongzhi, *Zhuan Falun* (Hong Kong: Falun Fo Fa, 1998), 349, 346; *Falun Dafa Yijie*, 25; *Zhuan Falun Fajie*, 27–28; *Zhuan Falun*, 346.

10. Li, *Zhuan Falun*, 348, 368–69; *Falun Fofa*, 4, 39, 82, 110, 85.

11. Li, *Falun Fofa*, 85–86, 4–5, 12; *Zhuan Falun*, 49–50; *Falun Buddha Law*, 50–51.

12. Li, *Falun Fofa*, 93; *Zhuan Falun Fajie*, 26, 64, 130; *Falun Buddha Law*, 16.

13. Li, *Falun Buddha Law*, 18–19, 20; *Zhuan Falun*, 21, 360.

14. Li, *Falun Buddha Law*, 44, 51.

15. Li, *Falun Fofa*, 6; *Falun Buddha Law*, 53–56.

16. Li, *Falun Buddha Law*, 29; Li Hongzhi, *China Falun Gong*, rev. ed. (Hong Kong: Falun Fo Fa, 1999), 185; *Zhuan Falun*, 306, 27, 265; *Falun Fofa*, 5, 8.

17. Li, *Falun Buddha Law*, 26. On another page (page 21) in the same book, however, Li seemed to think that humans were not important, dismissing them as being "simply too trivial."

18. Ibid., 62–63, 26; *Falun Dafa Yijie*, 58.

19. Li, *China Falun Gong*, 184–85; *Zhuan Falun*, 4, 68; *Falun Dafa Yijie*, 14, 58; *Zhuan Falun Fajie*, 314.

20. Li, *Zhuan Falun*, 70; *Falun Dafa Yijie*, 92.

21. Li, *Falun Buddha Law*, 61; *Zhuan Falun*, 17, 20.

22. Li, *Falun Buddha Law*, 28; *China Falun Gong*, 3; *Zhuan Falun*, 18–19.

23. Li, *Falun Buddha Law*, 27–28; *Zhuan Falun*, 18, 21; *Zhuan Falun Fajie*, 31.

24. Shaver, who died in 1975, was a prolific writer of science fiction whose career began with "I Remember Lemuria," published in the March 1945 issue of the popular sci-fi magazine *Amazing Stories*. Shaver offered what he claimed to be a true account of an ancient people who had survived the earth's destruction by going underground to live as the Deros. Shaver insisted that, unlike the rest of us, he was able to retain those prehistoric memories.

25. Li, *Falun Fofa*, 123.

26. Ibid., 22; Li, *China Falun Gong*, 2; *Falun Buddha Law*, 26; *Zhuan Falun*, 20; *Zhuan Falun Fajie*, 162; *Falun Fofa*, 89.

27. Li, *Falun Fofa*, 89, 14, 89–90.

28. Ibid., 90–91. Li, *Falun Buddha Law*, 52; *Zhuan Falun*, 60–61.

29. Li, *Falun Fofa*, 91, 92, 94; David Van Biema and Jaime A. FlorCruz, "The Man with the Qi," *Time*, May 10, 1999, p. 74; Rebecca Weiner, "Grassroots Conservatism Comes of (New) Age," *Tikkun* 15:1, January 2000, p. 9.

30. Li, *Falun Fofa*, 91–92; *Falun Buddha Law*, 87.

31. Li, *Falun Fofa*, 92–93.

32. Li, *Zhuan Falun*, 27; *Zhuan Falun Fajie*, 11.

33. Li, *Falun Fofa*, 2, 16; *Zhuan Falun*, 349, 53, 68, 14, 15; *China Falun Gong*, 173; *Zhuan Falun Fajie*, 15. Emphasis added.

34. Li, *Zhuan Falun*, i, ii; *Falun Buddha Law*, 53; Li Hongzhi, *Falun Dafa (Great Law of the Wheel)* (Hong Kong: Falun Fofa, 1999), 1–2.

35. Terry McCarthy and Mia Turner, "Inside the Falun Gong," *Time*, August 9, 1999, p. 50; Li, *Zhuan Falun*, 316, 380; *Zhuan Falun Fajie*, 272.

36. Li, *Falun Dafa Yijie*, 14, 196; *Zhuan Falun Fajie*, 216, 278, 14; *Falun Buddha Law*, 42.

37. Li, *Falun Fofa*, 35; *Falun Buddha Law*, 31.

38. Li, *Falun Fofa*, 59.

39. *Falun Dafa Yijie*, 51; *Zhuan Falun*, 30–31.

40. *Zhuan Falun*, 32; *Falun Buddha Law*, 9, 7, 30–31, 38–39.

41. Li, *Zhuan Falun*, 358; *Falun Dafa Yijie*, 89–90.

42. *Falun Dafa Yijie*, 24; *Falun Buddha Law*, 8–9; *China Falun Gong*, 139.

43. Li, *Zhuan Falun*, 358; *Zhuan Falun Fajie*, 63.

44. Li, *China Falun Gong*, 9; *Zhuan Falun Fajie*, 63; *Zhuan Falun*, 3; *Falun Buddha Law*, 39.

45. Li, *China Falun Gong*, 9.

46. *Falun Dafa Yijie*, 36; *Zhuan Falun*, 77.

47. Li, *Falun Buddha Law*, 86; *Zhuan Falun Fajie*, 228.

48. Li, *China Falun Gong*, 136; *Zhuan Falun*, 29, 312, 358, 67, 310.

49. Li, *Falun Buddha Law*, 88, 89, 86–87.

50. Ibid., 26; *Falun Dafa Yijie*, 36–37; *Zhuan Falun Fajie*, 252.

51. Li, *China Falun Gong*, 169.

52. Li, *Falun Buddha Law*, 30–31. 32; *Zhuan Falun*, 264, 2, 79.

53. *Falun Dafa Yijie*, 15–16. *Mo* means "the end"; *jie* actually refers to "kalpa"— another indication of Falun Gong's similarity to historical Chinese sectarian societies such as the White Lotus.

54. Li, *Zhuan Falun*, 30, 262.

55. Li, *Zhuan Falun Fajie*, 137, 64; *China Falun Gong*, 185; *Zhuan Falun*, 54, 68; *Falun Dafa Yijie*, 14; *Falun Fofa*, 2.

56. Li, *Zhuan Falun*, 309, 70; *Falun Buddha Law*, 7; *Falun Fofa*, 59–60.

57. Li, *Zhuan Falun*, 71; *Falun Buddha Law*, 9.

58. Li, *China Falun Gong*, 82.

59. McCarthy and Turner, "Inside the Falun Gong," 50.

60. Li, *China Falun Gong*, 171; *Zhuan Falun*, 29.

61. Li, *Zhuan Falun*, 331.

62. *Falun Dafa Yijie*, 182; *Zhuan Falun Fajie*, 15.

63. Li, *Zhuan Falun*, 28, 30–32, 27; *Falun Buddha Law*, 34.

64. Li, *China Falun Gong,* 147, 140, 169; *Falun Buddha Law,* 73, 75, 40; *Zhuan Falun,* 2, 79; *Falun Fofa,* 120; *Zhuan Falun Fajie,* 204.

65. Li, *Zhuan Falun,* 309, 28; *China Falun Gong,* 142.

66. Li, *Zhuan Falun,* 344, 54.

67. Ibid., 47, 50, 295, 366; Li, *China Falun Gong,* 173, 157, 172. Law bodies, according to Li, appear to the physical eye as a "shadow."

68. Li, *Zhuan Falun,* 64.

69. Li, *Zhuan Falun Fajie,* 109; *China Falun Gong,* 168, 177; *Falun Buddha Law,* 24; *Zhuan Falun,* 322–23, 66.

70. Li, *Zhuan Falun,* 22, 65; *Falun Dafa Yijie,* 21; *China Falun Gong,* 7, 8.

71. Li, *Zhuan Falun,* 48, 57, 323, 328–29. Li maintains that the "Buddha school" believes "there are eyes all over the body" because each pore on the human body is an eye. The Daoists, for their part, believe that each acupuncture point on the human body is an eye. See Li, *China Falun Gong,* 11–12.

72. Li, *Zhuan Falun,* 329–30.

73. Ibid., 40, 76; Li, *Zhuan Falun Fajie,* 39.

74. *Falun Dafa Yijie,* 22; *Zhuan Falun,* 330–31.

75. Li, *Falun Buddha Law,* 17, 39, 100; *Zhuan Falun,* 309, 54; *China Falun Gong,* 168, 143.

76. Li, *China Falun Gong,* 143; *Falun Buddha Law,* 91, 94.

77. *Falun Dafa Yijie,* 17; Christopher Hitchens, "For Whom the Gong Tolls," *Nation,* November 20, 2000, p. 9; Li, *China Falun Gong,* 133.

78. Li, *China Falun Gong,* 132, 82, 154.

79. Li, *Zhuan Falun,* 33, 54–55.

80. Li, *China Falun Gong,* 132–33.

81. Li, *Zhuan Falun Fajie,* 267–68, 163; *Falun Fofa,* 40.

82. Li, *Zhuan Falun Fajie,* 165–66, 138, 276, 157. That might explain why, according to Li, readers of his books find that the eyes in his photo inside the book seem alive and "follow" the reader.

83. Li, *Zhuan Falun Fajie,* 104; *China Falun Gong,* 154, 181; *Falun Buddha Law,* 1, 101.

84. Frank Ching, "Falun Gong: Giant vs. Ghost," *Far Eastern Economic Review,* February 22, 2001. Li, *China Falun Gong,* 167, 137, 139, 173; *Zhuan Falun,* 65; *Falun Buddha Law,* 9; *Falun Dafa Yijie,* 132.

85. Li, *Falun Fofa,* 56; *Zhuan Falun Fajie,* 317, 312, 329; *Falun Dafa Yijie,* 199.

86. Li, *Falun Fofa,* 60; *Falun Dafa Yijie,* 173–74; *Zhuan Falun,* 317–18; *Zhuan Falun Fajie,* 381; *Falun Fofa,* 56–57, 40; *Falun Dafa Yijie,* 23.

87. Li, *Zhuan Falun Fajie,* 175, 288; *Falun Dafa Yijie,* 200, 186.

88. As examples, see *Falun Dafa Yijie,* 5, 65, 80; Li, *Zhuan Falun,* 277, 318.
89. Li, *Falun Buddha Law,* 23; *Falun Fofa,* 14; *Zhuan Falun,* 37.
90. Li, *Zhuan Falun,* 354–55, 344.
91. *Falun Dafa Yijie,* 59; *Falun Buddha Law,* 83; *Zhuan Falun Fajie,* °
    4–5; *Zhuan Falun,* 354–56.
92. Li, *Falun Buddha Law,* 25, 58–60, 69, 86–87; *Zhuan Falun Fajie,* 4, 173;
    381–82.
93. Li, *Falun Buddha Law,* 58–59, 86.
94. Li, *Falun Dafa Yijie,* 135, 200, 28, 10; *Falun Fofa,* 34–36.
95. Li, *Falun Buddha Law,* 60–61.
96. Li, *Zhuan Falun Fajie,* 185, 205, 235. In spite of recognizing Christianity as a
    "proper religion," Li is critical of it because he "did not see Orientals in Jesus'
    heaven."
97. Li, *Falun Fofa,* 35; *Falun Buddha Law,* 60, 71; *Falun Dafa Yijie,* 113.
98. Li, *Zhuan Falun Fajie,* 85, 368, 231, 334; *Falun Buddha Law,* 3.

Chapter Four
The State vs. Falun Gong

1. "Officials, Employees of Central Organs Support Falun Gong Ban," *Xinhua
   News Agency* (hereafter *XNA*), July 23, 1999.
2. "Definitions of Terms: Cults, Sects and Denominations," www.Religious
   Tolerance.org.
3. Ibid.
4. Ibid.
5. "On the Evil Nature of Falun Gong," *People's Daily,* February 2, 2001.
6. Duan Qi, "Xiejiao di jiben tedian" (Basic Characteristics of Evil Cults), in
   *Falun Gong xianxiang pingxi (A Critical Analysis of the Falun Gong Phenom-
   enon)* (Beijing: shehui kexueh wenxian, 2001), 221–22.
7. Fu Fang, "Jingsheng kongzhi: Xiejiao di gongtong tedian" (Mind Control:
   The Common Charateristic of Evil Cults), in *Falun Gong xianxiang pingxi,*
   217–20.
8. "The Falun Gong Show," *Harper's Magazine,* October 1999, p. 18.
9. "Xinhua Releases Case Study on Falun Gong-ravaged Families," *XNA,*
   April 5, 2001.
10. "Falun Gong Tries to Cheat Western Public Opinion: Chinese Ambassador,"
    XNA, July 26, 2001.
11. "Falun Gong Scourges Mind, Body (3)," *XNA,* April 26, 2001; "Xinhua

Releases Case Study on Falun Gong-Ravaged Families," *XNA,* April 5, 2001; "Jin Guiqin, Former Head of Falun Gong Training Base," *XNA,* August 16, 1999; "Cases of Injury and Death Related to Falun Gong, Reported in Founder's Home Province," *XNA,* July 26, 1999.

12. "Cases of Injury and Death Related to Falun Gong."

13. "Falun Gong Scourges Mind, Body"; "On the Evil Nature of Falun Gong"; "Falun Gong Leads Its Followers to Homicides (1)," *XNA,* April 17, 2001.

14. "The Falun Gong Show"; "People's Daily Commentary on Falun Gong (2)," *XNA,* April 17, 2001; "Falun Gong Leads Its Followers to Homicides (2)," *XNA,* April 17, 2001; "China's Xinhua Carries Confession of Falun Gong Follower," BBC monitoring of a *XNA* report, January 25, 2002.

15. "Exhibition Focuses on Evil Nature of Cults," *China Daily* (hereafter *CD*), July 17, 2001.

16. "Analysis of Falun Gong Leader's Malicious Fallacies," *XNA,* July 23, 1999; "Police: Falun Gong Followers Leak State Secrets," *XNA,* October 25, 1999.

17. "Xinhua Commentary on Political Nature of Falun Gong," *XNA,* August 2, 1999; Yan Shi, *Shiji jupian Li Hongzhi (Fraud of the Century Li Hongzhi)* (Beijing: Dazong wenyi, 1999), 108–11.

18. Yan, *Fraud of the Century,* 103; "Analysis of Falun Gong Leader's Malicious Fallacies."

19. "Li Hongzhi Defrauds People of Money," *XNA,* August 6, 1999; "Analysis of Falun Gong Leader's Malicious Fallacies."

20. "New Evidence of Falun Gong Leader's Fraudulent Behavior Found," *XNA,* August 5, 1999; "On the Evil Nature of Falun Gong."

21. Yan, *Fraud of the Century,* 105; "Another Irrefutable Evidnece of Falun Gong's Anti-Humanity (1)," *XNA,* July 19, 2001.

22. "Analysis of Falun Gong Leader's Malicious Fallacies."

23. "China's Key Think Tank Explains Need to Ban Falun Gong," *XNA,* August 12, 1999.

24. "Analysis of Falun Gong Leader's Malicious Fallacies." "People's Daily Says Li Hongzhi's Fallacies Reflect Dangerous Political Aims," *XNA,* July 28, 1999.

25. "Police: Falun Gong Followers Leak State Secrets," *XNA,* October 25, 1999; "Falun Gong Cult Becomes a 'Reactionary Political Force,' " *CD,* October 11, 2000.

26. "Cult Leader Becomes Anti-China Tool (5)," *XNA,* April 17, 2000.

27. "Falun Gong Tries to Cheat Western Public Opinion: Chinese Ambassador." "Falun Gong Cult Becomes a 'Reactionary Political Force.' "

28. "Xinhua Commentary on Political Nature of Falun Gong."

29. "Analysis of Falun Gong Leader's Malicious Fallacies"; "Li Hongzhi, a Cult Leader with Evil Political Ambition," *XNA*, August 4, 1999.

30. "People's Daily Says Li Hongzhi's Fallacies Reflect Dangerous Political Aims"; "Xinhua Commentary on Political Nature of Falun Gong."

31. "Analysis of Falun Gong Leader's Malicious Fallacies"; "Xinhua Commentary on Political Nature of Falun Gong."

32. The Chinese government claims to have found a letter of appointment from Li in Shanxi Province; "Appointment Letter from Falun Gong Head Found," *XNA*, August 3, 1999; "Falun Gong Has Tight Organization," *XNA*, August 2, 1999; "Xinhua Commentary on Political Nature of Falun Gong."

33. Craig S. Smith, "Sect Clings to the Web in the Face of Beijing's Ban," *NYT*, July 5, 2001.

34. "Falun Gong Has Tight Organization."

35. "Falun Gong Is Well Organized: Insiders (1)," *XNA*, August 10, 1999.

36. "Jin Guiqin, Former Head of Falun Gong Training Base," *XNA*, August 16, 1999; "Falun Gong Is Well Organized: Insiders (1)."

37. "Cases of Injury and Death Related to Falun Gong, Reported in Founder's Home Province," *XNA*, July 26, 1999; "Xinhua Commentary on Political Nature of Falun Gong."

38. "Appointment Letter from Falun Gong Head Found," *XNA*, August 3, 1999.

39. Terry McCarthy and Mia Turner, "Inside the Falun Gong," *Time*, August 9, 1999, p. 48; Gong Yue, "Falun Gong shijian dizhen yu sisuo (The Shocking and Thought-Provoking Falun Gong Incident)," *Beijing zhichun* (*Beijing Spring*), no. 73, June 1999, p. 32.

40. McCarthy and Turner, "Inside the Falun Gong," 48; Yan, *Fraud of the Century*, 6.

41. "Li Hongzhi's Role in Illegal Gathering at Zhongnanhai (7)," *XNA*, August 13, 1999.

42. Ibid.

43. "Falun Gong Cult Becomes a 'Reactionary Political Force'"; "Cult Leader Becomes Anti-China Tool (5)"; Fu Fang, "Jingsheng kongzhi: Xiejiao di gongtong tedian" (Mind Control: The Common Charateristic of Evil Cults), in *Falun Gong xianxiang pingxi*, 220.

44. "Falun Gong Ban Legal, Based on People's Will: Spokesman," *People's Daily*, January 15, 2001.

45. Ibid.

46. Ibid.; "Xinhua Commentary on Political Nature of Falun Gong."

47. "Falun Gong Ban Legal, Based on People's Will: Spokesman."

48. "People's Daily Commentary on Falun Gong (2)." "Falun Gong Ban Legal, Based on People's Will: Spokesman."

49. "Cult Re-education Camp Opens to Foreign Media," *CD*, May 23, 2001. "Rumors vs. Reality: Falun Gong Re-education Camp Exposed to Foreign Media," *XNA*, May 23, 2001.

50. "Re-education Camp: Cult Members Transformed Heart and Soul," *CD*, June 12, 2001.

51. "Ex-practitioners Get New Life after Abjuration of Cult," *CD*, May 22, 2001.

52. "Exhibition Focuses on Evil Nature of Cults." "Former Practitioners Write Letter to Ministry of Justice," *CD*, July 29, 2001.

53. "Falun Gong Ban Legal, Based on People's Will: Spokesman." "Falun Gong Tries to Cheat Western Public Opinion: Chinese Ambassador."

54. "Exhibition Focuses on Evil Nature of Cults."

Chapter Five
The Persecution of Other Faiths

1. *The Constitution of the People's Republic of China* (Beijing: Foreign Languages Press, 1983), 5; Articles 1 and 2 of *The Criminal Law and The Criminal Procedure Law of China* (Beijing: Foreign Languages Press, 1984), 9.

2. *Constitution of the People's Republic of China*, 33, 39.

3. Introduction in *People's Republic of China: The Crackdown on Falun Gong and Other So-Called "Heretical Organizations"* (Amnesty International Report, March 23, 2000), 3.

4. Ibid., 3.

5. As an example, at the 1998 meeting of the NPC, 200 out of a total of 2,949 delegates dissented on the appointment of Li Peng to the premiership, and 36 delegates opposed Jiang Zemin being both president of the PRC and chairman of the Central Military Commission. *Shijie ribao* (*World Journal*), March 16, 1998, p. A1.

6. "The Crackdown on 'Heretical Organizations,'" in *People's Republic of China*, 8.

7. Ben Dolven, "Prosecuting the Defence," *Far Eastern Economic Review* (hereafter *FEER*), December 13, 2001; Introduction in *People's Republic of China*, 2.

8. Franz Michael, "Law: A Tool of Power," in Yuan-li Wu, Franz Michael, John F. Copper, Ta-ling Lee, Maria Hsia Chang, and A. James Gregor, *Human Rights in the People's Republic of China* (Boulder: Westview, 1988), 50.

9. Shixiong Li and Xiqiu (Bob) Fu, eds., *Religion and National Security in China: Secret Documents From China's Security Sector* (Bayside, N.Y.: Committee for Investigation on Persecution of Religion in China, February 11, 2002), 4–6. The committee is an American organization that supports religious rights.

10. Foreword, in ibid.; Introduction in *People's Republic of China,* 1.

11. See "The Shadow," in Murray Stein, *Jung On Evil* (Princeton: Princeton University Press, 1995), 95–97.

12. "On the Evil Nature of Falun Gong," *People's Daily,* February 2, 2001. Duan Qi, "Xiejiao di jiben tedian" (Basic Characteristics of Evil Cults), and Fu Fang, "Jingsheng kongzhi: Xiejiao di gongtong tedian" (Mind Control: The Common Charateristic of Evil Cults) in *Falun Gong xianxiang pingxi (A Critical Analysis of the Falun Gong Phenomenon)* (Beijing: Shehui kexueh wenxian, 2001), 221–22, 217–20.

13. See the account by Zheng Yi in *Scarlet Memorial* (Boulder: Westview, 1996).

14. See Jean-Louis Margolin's account in the English translation (by Jonathan Murphy and Mark Kramer) of Nicolas Werth, Jean-Louis Panne, Andrzej Paczkowski, Karel Bartosek, and Jean-Louis Margolin, *The Black Book of Communism: Crimes, Terror, Repression* (Cambridge: Harvard University Press, 1999), 463–46.

15. As examples of political dissidents, Xu Wenli, Wang Youcai, and Qin Yongmin were sentenced to thirteen, twelve, and eleven years, respectively. They were part of a group of several hundred activists who, beginning in June 1998, tried to register the China Democracy Party in fourteen provinces and cities. John Pomfret, "China Widens Its Crackdown on Speech," *San Francisco Chronicle* (hereafter *SFC*), December 24, 1998, p. A10. In fact, the evidence seems to indicate that it is precisely the unknown who are imprisoned and abused. The more famous an individual, the more likely the Communist Party will be constrained in its behavior. This suggests that the outside world, including governments and such NGOs as Amnesty International, can have an important impact on the fates of those caught in Beijing's maw.

16. *World Journal,* March 30, 1998, p. A7. Nicholas D. Kristof, "God and China," *New York Times* (hereafter *NYT*), November 26, 2002.

17. Deng, "Speech at the Opening Ceremony of the National Conference on Science," and "Report on the Revision of the Constitution of the Communist Party of China," in *Deng Xiaoping: Speeches and Writings,* (New York: Pergamon, 1984), 52, 53, 149, 27, 33, 6, 5, 28.

18. Minxin Pei, "The Roots of China's Corruption," *FEER,* February 15, 2001.

19. Terry McCarthy and Mia Turner, "Inside the Falun Gong," *Time,* August 9, 1999, p. 48.

20. "Worried in Beijing," *Economist* (U.S.), August 7, 1999, p. 14; Frank Ching, "Falun Gong: Giant vs. Ghost," *FEER,* February 22, 2001; Richard Madsen, "Demystifying Falun Gong," *Current History,* September 2000, p. 245.

21. For example, many U.S. cities, including some in New Jersey, Texas, and California, have passed resolutions in support of Falun Gong and condemning the Chinese government's treatment of believers.

22. Jay Nordlinger, "Crackdown Time: Why Beijing Fears the Falun Gong," *National Review,* September 27, 1999, p. 24.

23. Charles Hutzler, "Beijing's Assaults Appear Successful in Breaking Down Spiritual Group," *Wall Street Journal* (hereafter *WSJ*) April 26, 2001.

24. "Worried in Beijing," 14; "China's Trial of Faith," *Economist,* November 6, 1999, p. 42.

25. "China's WTO Entry Spells Layoffs," *Lateline News,* November 2, 2001.

26. "Thousands of Oil Workers Stage Pension Protest in Northeast China," Deutsche Presse-Agentur (hereafter DPA), March 5, 2002.

27. Bruce Gilley, "How to Build a Rebellion," *FEER,* November 29, 2001.

28. "Police Clash with 1,000 Farmers Protesting Corruption in China," Agence France Presse (hereafter AFP), July 30, 2001; "Chinese Court Frees Sentenced Farmers," *Lateline News,* November 2, 2001.

29. "China's Peasants Unprepared for Shock Waves of WTO Membership," AFP, September 24, 2001; "Cutting Income Gaps Vital to China's Stability, Jiang Says," DPA, February 5, 2002; and Gilley, "How to Build a Rebellion."

30. "China's WTO Entry Spells Layoffs." "China's Peasants Unprepared for Shock Waves."

31. Hard figures of China's floating population are difficult to come by. Erik Eckholm of the *New York Times* estimated the total to be "upward of 100 million" at the end of 2001. See Erik Eckholm, "Low-Cost Schools in China Under Threat of Closure," *SFC,* November 4, 2001, p. A17. Citing Chinese government statistics, Taiwan scholar Fang Shan maintained that China's internal migrant labor exceeds 200 million people. See Fang Shan, "Dalu

chengshi nongmingong pinkun wenti" (The Poverty Problem of Peasant La-borers in Mainland Cities), *Zhongguo dalu yanjiu (Mainland China Studies)* 42:11, November 1999, p. 38.

32. Bruce Gilley, "Toil and Trouble," *FEER*, August 16, 2001.

33. "Cutting Income Gaps Vital to China's Stability." John Pomfret, "In China, the Rich Seek to Become the 'Big Rich,'" *Washington Post*, February 5, 2002.

34. Jiang Xueqin, "Fighting to Organize," *FEER*, September 6, 2001.

35. The study was conducted by Wang Gan, who studied the wealthy in Shen-zhen for her doctoral thesis at Yale University. See Pomfret, "In China, the Rich Seek to Become the 'Big Rich.' "

36. "China Briefing," *FEER*, December 13, 2001; "Senior Official Charged over USD 150 Million Graft Case," AFP, September 11, 2001; Pomfret, "In China, the Rich Seek to Become the 'Big Rich.' "

37. McCarthy and Turner, "Inside the Falun Gong," 48.

38. Philip P. Pan, "China Destroys Churches in Christmas Crackdown on Reli-gion," *SFC*, December 19, 2000, p. A20. Christopher Bodeen, "China's Unofficial Churches Draw Worldwide Attention," *SFC*, February 17, 2002, p. A14. Editorial, "Caesar's Realm," *FEER*, December 27, 2001.

39. Introduction to *People's Republic of China*. "U.S. Panel Says China Intensifies Crackdown on Religion," Reuters, May 1, 2001. Shixiong Li, "An Introduc-tion: Religious Freedom and the Chinese House Churches," in *People's Re-public of China*.

40. Kristof, "God and China."

41. Pan, "China Destroys Churches."

42. "China Goes on Offensive against Spiritual Groups Similar to Falun Gong," AFP, April 18, 2001. "Crackdown on 'Heretical Organizations,' " 16; "China Unearths New 'Evil Cult' and Saves Brainwashed Children," AFP, June 1, 2001.

43. "China Goes on Offensive"; "Crackdown on 'Heretical Organizations,' " 16.

44. In March 2001, a court in Liaoning province sentenced the leader of the White Sun Religion to twelve years in prison for allegedly raping women during his "healing" sessions. "China Sentences Cult Leader to 12 Years in Prison for Raping Women," AFP, March 6, 2001; "China Cracked Down Mao Worshipper," *Lateline News*, September 27, 2001.

45. "Crackdown on 'Heretical Organizations,' " 8. "Catholic Frees Catholic Bishop, Vatican News Agency Says," AFP, August 3, 2001. "Vatican Says China Detaining Many Priests," *SFC*, February 15, 2002, p. A10.

46. "Document One: The Ministry of Public Security of the People's Republic of China," in *Religion and National Security in China*. "Two Indicted on 'Cult' Charges in China, Rights Group Says," BBC monitoring, January 31, 2002.

47. "Document One: The Ministry of Public Security of the People's Republic of China," 9.

48. Ibid., 11.

49. Ibid.

50. Ibid.

51. "Document Seven: The Public Security Bureau of Beijing," in *Religion and National Security in China*.

52. Bodeen, "China's Unofficial Churches Draw Worldwide Attention," A14. In September 2002, probably in response to American pressure, an appeals court in central China overturned the death sentences of Gong and four other sect leaders citing lack of evidence. The following month, the five were retried: Gong and two sect leaders were sentenced to life in prison for rape and battery; the two remaining leaders were given fifteen-year sentences on the same charges. Christopher Bodeen, "Sect Leader in China Convicted of Rape," *SFC*, October 11, 2002, p. A10.

53. "Document One: The Ministry of Public Security of the People's Republic of China," 11; "Crackdown on 'Heretical Organizations,'" 10.

54. "Document Three: The Office of the Public Security Bureau of Anhui Province" and "Document Six: The 'Real God' Cult: Their Activities and Work Requirement," in *Religion and National Security in China*.

55. "Crackdown on 'Heretical Organizations,'" 12.

56. "Document One: The Ministry of Public Security of the People's Republic of China."

57. Ibid.

58. Ibid.

59. Ibid.

60. Ibid.

61. Ibid.; "Crackdown on 'Heretical Organizations,'" 15.

62. "China Goes on Offensive." "China Sect Leader Gets 12-Year Sentence," *SFC*, September 19, 2001, p. B4.

63. "Document One: The Ministry of Public Security of the People's Republic of China."

64. "China Reports Two Million Failed Suicides Annually," DPA, October 30, 2001.

65. Jay Nordlinger, quoting Robert Thurman, in "Crackdown Time," 24.

66. McCarthy and Turner, "Inside the Falun Gong," 49.

67. Ibid., 50.

68. "They Cannot Lock Up Hearts," *Newsweek International,* August 2, 1999, p. 42.

69. "Worried in Beijing," 14.

70. Ian Johnson, "A Blind Eye: China's Rigid Policies on Religion Helped Falun Dafa for Years," *WSJ,* December 13, 2000, p. A1. Christopher Hitchens, "For Whom the Gong Tolls," *Nation,* November 20, 2000, p. 9.

71. From the time of Qin Shihuang's unification to the Revolution of 1911 that ended dynastic rule, China's periods of unification and of fragmentation totaled 1,700 years and 900 years, respectively. Zhu Songbo, ed., *Fenlie guojia di hudong guanxi* (*Mutually Interactive Relationship of Divided States*) (Taipei: Institute of International Relations, 1989), 1–6.

72. "Echoes of Tiananmen," *Newsweek,* August 2, 1999, p. 6.

INDEX